FACTS AND OPINIONS
ON THE ISSUES OF OUR TIME

BOOK III

By

Dr. Mark L. Hopkins

PREFACE

When I wrote books I and II of "Facts and Opinions on the Issues of our Time," I wasn't sure there would ever be a Book III. Yet, here it is. The column, which is called Southern Perspective, continues to run on Sundays in the Anderson Independent-Mail, Anderson, SC, and in the newspapers of the GateHouse Media syndication. The syndication covers 37 states and 555 newspapers. An American proverb says, "From little acorns do mighty oaks grow." That certainly is the case with Southern Perspective, which just a decade ago was a new column each Sunday in one newspaper.

Responses from the community of readers are both surprising and gratifying. I say gratifying because I love getting comments on the column each week; surprising, because I can never predict what someone is going to say about something I have written. Often, a comment will reveal a perspective that, even after researching the subject, I did not expect.

The columns have been identified as "commentaries" on the world, the country, and the south. Topics generally come from the headlines of yesterday's newspaper, though I do have some pet topics such as education and religion. I have a particular penchant for history and tend to see everything from the perspective of what happened before that brought us to this point and where are we headed now.

By profession, I am a lifelong educator. I taught in junior high, high school, and at the college level. Today, in semi-retirement, I write. The column gets a goodly amount of my time, but in between I have written eight books. They are "Facts and Opinions," books I, II, & III, "Journey to Gettysburg," "The Wounds of War," "The World as it was When Jesus Came," "On the Road with Paul the Apostle," and "Pirates, Privateers, and the U.S. Navy." Most are still available at Amazon.com and Barnes & Noble.

A number of people have helped me develop the column. These include former Independent-Mail Editor Bonnie Williams, who taught me much about how to keep it short and to the point.

Kylie Yerka often dressed up my column with pictures and has helped with publication of the column books. Most significantly is my wife, Ruth, who critiques everything I write and, often, has advice that adds texture and makes them hit closer to home.

It is my wish that readers have the opportunity to read, think, and then respond if the spirit moves. The author can be reached by email at presnet@presnet.net and welcomes the opportunity for intelligent debate. Who knows, we might both learn something.

TABLE OF CONTENTS

SECTION 13: OTHER 215

1

NATIONAL ISSUES

Every generation has its own challenges and 2018 is no different. The last presidential election crystalized a number of the key issues of our time. Some of these include border security, health care, immigration, gender equality, minimum wage, and the environment.

Long standing issues such as welfare, social security, and drug use, gave way to debates on guns and the 2nd Amendment, refugees, and military threats such as North Korea and ISIS. High cost issues such as renewing our infrastructure and revamping our education system always seem to be discussed but put off for future consideration, generally because the money is not readily available. It seems that everywhere we look we have a new challenge.

History tells us that it has always been so. In the 1700s we had the Revolutionary War and the creation of a Constitution for a different kind of government than the world had ever seen. The 1800s brought us a Civil War where we fought brother against brother for the soul of our country, to be either slave or free. In the 1900s we fought four wars and had a great economic recession.

In past years we have always found a champion to lead us in times of peril. Names like George Washington, Abraham Lincoln, Woodrow Wilson, Franklin Roosevelt, Dwight Eisenhower, and Ronald Reagan stand out in the pages of our history books. Will we find new leaders for the challenges of the 21st Century? Doubtless, they are preparing for leadership even as this is being written. Who will step forward to bring us together as a country, to meet the challenges of a new century? Time and history will tell.

It is fitting that the first section of this book should focus on National Issues. The readers of history tomorrow will judge us today on how we handle the issues of our time.

AMERICA'S MANAGEMENT GURUS INFLUENCE THE WORLD: UNFORTUNATELY, NOT THE U.S. GOVERNMENT

Every business major at our colleges and universities knows the names of U.S. business gurus W. Edwards Deming, Peter Drucker, and Peter Covey. If you add in the name of Peter Pyhrr you have a full spread of the major management theorists who have influenced how business and industrial management has been conducted in the United States over the past seventy years.

Deming gave us his theory called "Total Quality Management" back in the late 1940s and early 1950s. Peter Drucker added "Management by Objectives," Peter Covey focused on the "habits and practices of effective business and industrial leaders," and Peter Pyhrr believed that all budgeting for organizations should start each year at zero. Thus, "Zero Based Budgeting." Many other researchers and theorists have written on the subject of management but almost all fit into the categories of one or the other of the "major" four listed above.

> **"If you want something new, you have to stop doing something old."**
>
> Peter Drucker

At the end of World War II, business in the U.S. was growing faster than management could keep up. To meet the challenge of handling business and industry with larger numbers of people, a new wave of management theorists began to influence how U.S. business and industry was managed. In all areas of business, technology, education, etc. the United States shared its expertise with virtually every country on the planet.

It is a rare business or industry that has not been visited by leaders from Japan, China, and many other places over the past half century. During my years as a community college President I often found myself in front of a tour group from some foreign country who had come to learn how we were doing "it" in the United States. We have also watched enrollments of international students at our graduate schools swell to more than a million students. What we know and how we do things continues to be the standard for the world.

We do pay a price for sharing our knowledge and expertise with the world. The manufacture of steel, automobiles, textiles, and a number of other commodities which used to be the foundation of business/industry in the U.S. is now spread across the globe. Today, it is a rare automobile that one can identify as having been "made in the U.S.A." In virtually all, at least some part of the finished vehicle has been made outside our country. The same is true with other products. For a time every country in the world seemed to be copying us. It hasn't changed. We still know how to run businesses and organizations better than anyone else in the world though others are gaining on us.

Knowing what to do and how to do it, doesn't mean we are doing it in all key aspects of our country. Despite the obvious expertise available, the U.S. government continues to operate much as it did a century ago. Note the U.S. Senate with a hundred attorneys closing the doors of the Senate and authoring a health bill with no input from the health professions. Note a President whose primary advisors are four former military generals who has just sent a major tax code revision to Congress without involving any of the gurus of the U.S. economy. Note the actions from the White House that have radically changed our efforts to preserve the environment without listening to the advice of the experts in that field.

If our Washington DC leadership was enrolled in any of our university graduate business management programs they would be earning no better than a "D" grade for their efforts so far. They may well know what they want to accomplish but they have shown themselves to be inept at making it happen. Peter Drucker, the first of the major 20th century management gurus said, "If you want something new, you have to stop doing something old."

AND THE BAND PLAYED ON

Randy Shilts wrote a book about the Aids epidemic and used that title. The classic book and movie "Titanic" could also have been called by that same title. It is hard to forget the scene in the "Titanic" movie where the band continued to play even as the ship slipped into the depths of the ocean.

When the Titanic hit that iceberg it was sailing at top speed through waters dotted with ice bergs while the people on board continued to dance and party, seemingly oblivious to the dangers in the water just a few yards away. That illustration pretty well defines the United States over the past thirty years. We have been sailing along at top speed through dangerous waters continuing to dance and party while danger continues to haunt our country in a variety of ways.

> ## "When will we learn, when will we ever learn."
>
> Line from an
> American folk song

It is a short trip from the AIDS epidemic and the Titanic to the governmental strife we are experiencing in Washington D.C. The list of hazards are long and significant as they relate to preserving our way of life. Check the following examples from that very long list.

- Our country is continuing to spend more money each month than we take in. The national debt continues to grow. At some point there will be a great reckoning.
- We have multiple environmental challenges, the latest is how to take advantage of new energy sources provided by technology advances. We can celebrate our energy breakthrough but the by-products that need remediation are the potential of fouling our drinking water and the underground aquifer that has supplied our mid-western farms with water for generations. We should also point out that earthquakes follow the fracking industry with the state of Oklahoma is a prime example. They had more than 100 earthquakes last year. Global warming continues to be a serious issue.

- The infrastructure of the United States, the bridges, roads, national parks, water and sewer systems, are in such disrepair that they are nearing emergency status. Note the drinking water problems in Flint, Michigan which our experts tell us is just the tip of the iceberg.
- When most of the national pundits are asked about the actions/in-actions of Congress they use one word to describe the situation, "gridlock." With a long backlist of issues to deal with they insist on tilting at windmills. The votes to abolish Obamacare now number more than fifty. The last two sessions of Congress were the least productive in history. One hundred days into the new administration and nothing appears to have changed.

All of this and more, "as the band played on." The U.S. government has been involved in borrowing against the future with an underfunded Social Security fund, budget shortfalls that don't get made up, and entering high cost conflicts abroad that are funded by borrowing yet more from our grandchildren. We used to call this dilemma "guns versus butter." In short, if we had to buy guns we couldn't afford butter. Since the presidency of Lyndon Johnson we have had a total of more than twenty years of foreign conflicts from Viet Nam to Iraq to Afghanistan to Syria. All of this while actually lowering taxes. In short, we bought both guns and butter and borrowed the money from our grandchildren to pay for them.

The new congress is once again is focused on lowering taxes. Some say that cutting taxes causes the economy to heat up to the benefit of all. Unfortunately, that belief is not born out by history. In truth, history tells us just the opposite. The more taxes the better the economy and the less growth of the national debt. As old Casey Stengle, former manager of the New York Yankees used to say, "You could look it up."

"And the band played on?" Oh yes. What is that line in an old folk song? "When will we ever learn, when will we ever learn." History speaks, we should listen.

AN IMPLOSION IS COMING

As most who read my column each week know, I write much about history but am averse to making predictions. However, this one time I am going to make an exception. The Chinese have a proverb that says, "If we don't change the direction we are headed, we will end up where we are going." Well, we are headed for trouble and when it comes it will be political and constitutional, as well as social.

Three factors predict a major governmental implosion. They are 1) presidential approval ratings, 2) management/administrative theory and 3) national level demonstrations. The following will provide some clarification.

> **"If we don't change the direction we are headed, we will end up where we are going."**
>
> Chinese proverb

President Trump's approval ratings, at 45 percent when he was sworn in, have now dipped to less than 40 percent by reputable polling organizations. No modern president has had such low ratings at the beginning of his presidency. This, during his "honeymoon" period. To add to his woes, women disapprove of his presidency at the 63 percent level. Minorities overwhelmingly disapprove at a 79 percent rate. The youth (under thirty) disapprove at a 69 percent rate. The majority white population disapproves at a 46 percent level.

Management theorist such as Peter Drucker, Stephen Covey and John Kenneth Galbrith, three well known writers on the subject, have stated over and over that organizations are managed with the consent of the governed. In business or governmental organizations much of the cause of organizational difficulty is related to a low level of support by those governed. When disapproval rises above 20 percent, trouble is coming. Need-less-to-say disapproval ratings for the current administration in Washington DC are double and triple that benchmark 20 percent number.

Being President of the United States is the most difficult job in the world. In a recent speech President Trump stated that he "inherited a mess." He was right. The U.S. presidency has and will always be a mess. Not only do we have a very diverse population that makes great demands on its leadership, the U.S. president is almost by fiat the leader of the free world. And, like the United States, the world is a mess, only worse.

Presidential elections seldom give a president more than a few percentage points above 50 percent of the vote. In this last election it was less than 50 percent. Early in the tenure of a new president it is necessary to take action to placate the opposition, to gain enough support to allow him/her to govern with majority support. That is, seemingly, not in the current administration's plan.

Negative ratings mean little unless the disapproval translates into action. Do we have evidence of such action? In January we had a march on Washington by an estimated crowd of more than two million women demonstrating about policies related to their concerns. Minorities are demonstrating all across the country about immigration policies. On Presidents' Day "Not my President" rallies sprang up in dozens of cities nationwide. Youthful demonstrators are showing their disapproval on college campuses. In short, we have not had so much turmoil on the national scene since the anti-Viet Nam War demonstrations of the late 1960s. Then, government literally stopped while we straightened out our mess. Nixon won the presidency in 1968 promising to end the Viet Nam War and quell the demonstrations.

Predictions, like this column, are just words on a paper. However, these particular words come from one who taught both history and government, who administered public organizations for a career, and has been an interested observer of the national political scene for more than sixty years. The way to keep from getting where we are headed is for our president and his leadership team to realize that one governs with the consent and support of the governed. Without that support a president may continue in office but for all practical purposes his presidency will be over before it is hardly started.

BENGHAZI

Everyone agrees the death of Ambassador Christopher Stevens and three of his staff members in Benghazi, Libya was a tragedy. That includes Democrats, Republicans and virtually everyone else who knows anything about the attack on our Embassy that fateful night in 2012. Everyone also agrees that being an Ambassador in a foreign Embassy is a dangerous responsibility.

Recent U.S. history tells us that seven Ambassadors have been killed while on duty over the past fifty years: John Gordon Mein, Guatemala, 1968; Cleo Noel Jr., Sudan, 1973; Rodger Davies, Cyprus, 1974; Francis Mallory, Lebanon, 1976; Adolph Dubs, Afghanistan, 1979; Laurence Foley, Jordan, 2002; Christopher Stevens, Libya, 2012.

Seven ambassadors have been killed while on duty over the past fifty years.

Multiple other attacks have occurred around the globe on American Embassies where people were killed, just not the Ambassador. Our latest loss, Ambassador Stevens, occurred during the watch of President Obama and Sec. of State Hillary Clinton. Assigning blame for Stevens' death has been the subject of the Benghazi hearings on Capitol Hill in Washington D.C. in October. (To my knowledge this is the first hearing for this purpose related to any of the tragic deaths of Ambassadors.)

In order to understand what happened and why, let's have a look at history and International Law. Virtually every country in the world has Embassies in other countries. The United States alone has more than 250. These international efforts at relationships between countries are coordinated by The United Nations. There are several "constants" with all such Embassies.

- Embassies can be established when both countries desire to make such arrangements.
- Security of the outside of an Embassy is the responsibility of the host nation.

- Security of the inside of an Embassy is the responsibility of the visiting nation.
- The grounds and buildings of an Embassy are judged by international law to be the property of the visiting nation and are considered to be a part of that visiting nation.
- Construction of such compounds is the responsibility of the host nation. (When the most recent U.S. Embassy facility in Moscow was created we found so many hidden listening devices that we judged the facility to be unusable.)
- The diplomats assigned to Embassies by the visiting nation are under the laws of their own country and have diplomatic immunity from arrest in the host country.

Security of our personnel is the primary focus of the Benghazi hearings. In past years I have visited many U.S. Embassies in Asia. When I visited our facility in Beijing, China I was struck by the external security provided by the host nation. At each corner of the compound there was a guard building and there was an almost constant marching of Chinese troops around the outside of the facility. I counted 48 guards on duty just outside the grounds.

In virtually every instance where we have lost diplomatic personnel to Embassy attacks the external security of the facility, the responsibility or the host nation, was lacking. That was certainly true in Benghazi where reports reveal that the external defense force disappeared prior to the attack and five Marines attempted to defend the compound against, literally, hundreds of heavily armed attackers.

Was Hillary Clinton responsible for leaving Ambassador Stevens and his staff under-defended? How much security personnel is enough when the Embassy Compound is to be defended by the host nation? Should Colin Powell, Madeline Albright, Cyrus Vance, Henry Kissinger, and Dean Rusk, all Secretaries of State during previous tragedies, have been held responsible for the deaths of the other Ambassadors from 1968 until now? Who were the presidents during those other tragedies and what was their responsibility? Where does the money come from to defend our turf in other countries?

The most recent hearings are the third on the Benghazi tragedy. What else is to be learned by continuing to beat this dead horse?

BUT, I HEARD IT
THROUGH THE GRAPEVINE

It may sound preposterous but it's true
Cause I heard it through the grapevine.
And Friend, I'm about to lose my mind
Cause I heard it through the grapevine.

That song was written in 1966 by Norman Whitfield and Barrett Strong for Motown Records. The message was about "hearsay." The 2017 version of the grapevine is the Internet. According to the FBI and the CIA, fake news items that have appeared on the Internet in recent months seem to have been given credence by a significant portion of the population. "Oh, no one believes that 'stuff.'" No? Well try the following.

Hillary and Bill Clinton are running a child sex slave ring from a Pizza Hut in Washington DC. Does that sound ridiculous? Well, a man from North Carolina showed up there and fired off his gun inside the restaurant because he believed it. Earlier, two women came to investigate the tunnel under the restaurant reportedly used to hide the children. The restaurant has received numerous threats both by phone and by E-mail.

It may sound preposterous but it's true
cause I read it on the ....Internet.

President Obama was born in Kenya so he couldn't be a legitimate president. That one has been repeated so often that it is now being used by the news media as an example of an untruth said often enough that it become believable. Is it true? No. It has been debunked over and over. Even Donald Trump said that it wasn't true in a speech back in November. Still, polls show that more than 30% of our population seems convinced. Folks, his mother was from Kansas.

And friend, I'm about to lose my mind
Cause I read it on the ....Internet.

The murder rate in the U.S. is the highest it has been in 45 years. In fact, it is near a 50-year low. This, despite the problems in Chicago.

Britney Spears died. No, Britney is alive and well and planning her next concert.

But the rumor must be true

Cause I read it on the ....Internet.

The fake news items generally appear through Face Book or some other Social Media unit and go viral. One poll said that more people believe the fake news posts than believe the newspapers.

Let's examine that last statement. Virtually anyone with a computer can put something on Face Book. There is no fact check, no way to verify the relative truth of the statement, no consequences if the presentation is found to be libelous, self-serving, or damaging to someone else. Newspapers, on the other hand

Hillary and Bill Clinton are running a child sex slave ring.

have both ethics and standards for their articles. Virtually every news article is required to have two sources in order to be presented as factual. And, if you feel harmed in any way you can sue a newspaper for damages. You have no such remedy on Face Book.

The year 2016 was a difficult year for fake news. Candidates from both sides of the aisle were attacked with items that had no foundation in fact. Over and over statements were debunked. Awards were given for "One, two or three Pinocchio's." And, if it was really bad they called it "Pants on fire." Still, if a portion of the voting public believed it, the fake news worked. Because it did we can expect more of the same in future elections.

What do we do about such? We are long overdue for a "governor" on Face Book and other social media. Just as political candidates must take credit/blame for advertisements on Radio and TV, (My name is_____ and I approved this message.) the same should apply to social media. No one should be able to get away with attacking a person's good name, causing a business to fail, or attempting to steal an election without paying a cost for the violation.

GOOD NEWS AT THE END OF 2017

We are nearing the first anniversary of Donald Trump's inauguration as our President. Most would attest to the fact that this has been one of the most unusual first years by any President in memory. The nay-sayers have been out in force and if one believed what they say it would be easy to visualize that our 241 year experiment in democracy was nearing an end. However, this writer is not so pessimistic. To paraphrase Mark Twain, "Our demise has been greatly exaggerated."

I have been looking for that silver lining, that pot of gold at the end of the rainbow and I have found significant reason for optimism.

> ## "Our demise has been greatly exaggerated."
>
> Mark Twain

First, why are things so negative? We know that we are living in a time when public figures say terrible things about others, when fake news on face book seems to become reality, where deranged gunmen shoot innocent people who just happened to be at the wrong place at the wrong time. Such can happen anywhere at any time and we need to be constantly alert to potential problems.

Why is our news media loaded with bad news with not much good news to balance it? The reality of our news media is that they do not make the news. Instead, they report what others say and do. Unfortunately, much has been negative in our country over the past several months while our leaders in Washington DC have found it difficult to get their act together.

Here is some positive balance that, perhaps, has not been at the front of your mind. One must go back several years to get a true perspective on what is happening, which is why I have traced our nation's economic news back to 2008, a decade ago, to compare with our situation today.

- Unemployment: ... was 9.2 percent, is now 4.1 percent.
- Gasoline: ....was $2.69 per gallon nationwide, is now $2.48.

- National GDP growth: ....was -0.3%, is now + 3.7%.
- Growth of National Debt: .....was 1.65 trillion, is 555 billion.
- Stock Market: .....was 8,850, is now pushing 24,000.
- High School graduations reached 84 percent in 2017.
- Cancer Mortality has dropped 25 percent over the past 25 years.
- Issues related to terror are constantly with us, but ISIS is on the ropes, as is Al Qaeda.

So, shall we give President Trump credit for the improvements in our economic situation? Actually, presidents don't have much leverage when it comes to the economy. They can't tell business/industry how many people to hire or how many products to produce. We should remember that fact when President Trump is trying to fulfill his many campaign promises related to jobs and the economy. Rather than crediting the president for past successes in the economy, we should credit inventions and innovations in the oil industry and the wisdom of our leaders following the great depression who envisioned circumstances similar to what became reality in 2008 and set up regulations to forestall any repeat of that national disaster.

The polls tell us that at least half of our population is concerned about future actions of our president. We should not be overly worried. Much of what he promised to do during the campaign is not in the purview of the President. He may influence change but Congress has control of new laws and the budget. The Supreme Court is still the protector of the Constitution. Change may come but it will be slow and measured, much less so than political rhetoric would lead us to believe.

Some may call me an eternal optimist but, from my perspective, any good news is worth celebrating. The improvement in our economic, health, and graduation numbers should cause us all to pause here at the end of another year and be thankful for significant successes in a number of areas of national importance.

IS THE UNITED STATES IN DECLINE?

The Chinese "Epoch Times," a regional newspaper from Beijing says, "The United States as a super power is no more. China is in The Year of The Rooster. By the time it is over, the United States will be over as well."

That proclamation is not a surprise. China has become our chief competitor on the world stage and is obsessed with its own importance. In that communist country the decline of the U.S. is "the company line."

Still, many of our own prognosticators have said the U.S. is in decline. The Pew Research Center reported, "For the first time in American history it is predicted that our children will be less prosperous than their parents." In short, they say the foundation of our society, the U.S. economy, is in decline. To defend that position they point out that the 2% increase in our national GDP in recent year's shows a decline from our peak years of the 1950s when it regularly topped four percent. (GDP is short for Gross Domestic Product. The GDP is the value of all goods and services produced in the U.S. in a year.)

> "For the first time in American history it is predicted that our children will be less prosperous than their parents."
>
> Pew Research Center report

I beg to differ with those so-called experts. The U.S. has been the dominant country in the world since WWII, and we aren't going anywhere. There is much research to counterbalance the Pew report. I can envision a very different future than some of our more negative prognosticators and have the evidence to back it up. The wolf and warp of our GDP is certainly a predictive factor. However, the GDP by itself tells only a part of the story. The U.S. economy is a product of several factors beyond GDP, including two that are key. These are 1) technological advances and 2) population growth. Technological advances and population growth dictate the GDP.

The development of technology is on-going, We have more than 3000 colleges and universities across the country, each with research as a major responsibility. Clemson University, Georgia Tech, MIT, and most of the major graduate universities in the country value research as a major thrust of their institutions. To these efforts we can credit the productivity of our farms, industrial growth, computers, etc. It is not likely we will have less effort toward such development in the future.

Population, however, is a more difficult question. Population, still growing in the underdeveloped countries, has been in decline all over the world in the more industrialized countries. The four largest economies in the world are, in order 1) The United States, 2) China, 3) Japan, and 4) Germany. Japan and Germany have experienced population decline for several years. Germany is so concerned with their decline that they have taken in more than 600,000 Syrian refugees over the past three years to stem the tide. Japan projects losing one third of their population between now and 2060 despite major efforts to slow the decline. The United States and China continue to show modest gains in population. China has been concerned enough by the decline of the growth rate of their population that they have cancelled their "one-child" per family policy. The U.S. population has a declining birth rate which is a concern but we have held our own due to immigration which brings us approximately one million new citizens a year.

The current GDP in the United States is $59,000 per person. As long as new technology is being developed and the population continues to rise we can expect the per-person GDP to continue to rise as well. If our GDP growth rate stays ahead of our population growth we can expect the quality of life and the buying power of each household to continue to improve as well.

So, China is on the rise but so are we. To paraphrase the words of American writer Mark Twain, "The report of our demise has been greatly exaggerated."

SMART AS A COCKROACH?

Several million years ago scientist tell us that the world was dominated by dinosaurs. They died out following a massive collision with an asteroid eons ago. We know they existed because we keep digging up their bones in various places around the globe.

One of the curiosities of the search for pre-historic dinosaurs is that we often run across evidence of other species as well, most of them long since extinct. One of those not extinct, still to be found on virtually every continent in every city of the world, is the cockroach. Yes, we still have the cockroach who has survived millions of years while the world has changed radically many times.

The question for the human species, you and me, is "Are we as smart as a cockroach?" The primary attribute of the cockroach is that it is adaptable.

The primary attribute of a cockroach is that it is adaptable.

The world's climate has changed radically over the past several million years moving back and forth from periods of glacier to rain forest to desert conditions. Many species did not adapt well to the changes in climate and have died off. Not the Cockroach. That little varmint adapted to each new condition. In fact, the jury is still out but I'm betting it would find a way to live on the moon.

By contrast, we humans hate change. Change as we all know causes conflict and the greater the change the greater the conflict. So, what has changed in recent years? Here are three examples from a very long list.

- Minorities now make up more than 50 percent of all births in the United States each year and our public school population is now more than 50 percent minority.
- The states of Texas, Colorado, and Arizona, long a part of the Republican right, have the fastest growing minority populations in the country and will most likely begin to vote on the other side of the political isle sooner rather than later.

- The Supreme Court ruling has changed marriage laws and at least a part of our population is confused as to who is a wife, a husband or a partner.

So, what can we anticipate will be the next major change for us: driverless cars, a cure for cancer, robots in the home, a women in the White House?

Obviously, change is on-going and conflict will be a continuing way of life. No matter how much we might like things to be the way they used to be, that ship has sailed.

That brings us back to the cockroach. That little varmint has proven itself to be the most adaptable creature God ever made. It has withstood all kinds of change and has thrived against conditions that even the dinosaurs could not withstand. So, the question for us is, "Are we as smart as a cockroach?"

THE STATE OF THE UNION, 2018

Here we are in 2018, a full year after Donald Trump became our new President, and the world hasn't come to an end, yet.

Those who predicted gloom and doom have been proven to be half right. We have had plenty of gloom. The doom, well, as Mark Twain predicted, "The reports of my (our) demise were greatly exaggerated."

So, what is good and what is not so good. Let's take a look at the state of the union. Well, at least, let's take a look from one person's perspective. On the bright side.......

The stock market is at an all-time high at 26,000+ and still going up. That is a 30 percent increase over the past year and more than 120 percent in a decade. Big investors are making money hand over fist.

Those who predicted gloom and doom have been proven to be half right.

Gas prices are slightly lower over the past year and hover nationally at around $2.54 a gallon. That is more than a 25 percent reduction over a decade ago and has held steady now for more than eighteen months. That computes to about $500 in savings for the average motorist over a twelve month period.

Unemployment is at the historically low rate of 4.2 percent. Economist tell us that 5 percent is full employment. A portion of our work force is constantly unemployed because of technological advancements in the marketplace. Some are what we term "hard core," unemployed but most cycle back into the work force with additional training.

From the not so good perspective we have a more disquieting history in the recent past.

Illegal immigration continues to be a major national issue. We are not alone in having that problem to solve. Most of Europe is facing the same dilemma. The DACA vote looms and 800,000 lives hang in the balance.

We are still at war in the mid-east and it seems to be heating up again with a recent surge of troops. It is a quagmire and just as we seem to have extricated ourselves from that mess, we get pulled back in again. Can we never anticipate "Peace on earth, good will toward men?" Our President has some "wins" and some "losses" during his first year in office, not dissimilar to most of his predecessors. The thing that is very different is his constant popularity ratings which hover between thirty and forty percent, well below presidents all the way back to Lincoln's time. Those low ratings do not bode well for future successes in Congress nor Republican success in the 2018 elections.

Perhaps the most disappointing thing is the constant attack on the news media from the President. New words and phrases such as, "fake news," "alternate facts," and, "the enemy," have entered our vocabulary. His most recent speech delivered in Europe at the World Economic Forum contained these lines, "How nasty, how mean, how vicious, and how false the news can be." Expecting some support from other heads of state he, instead, got hisses and boos.

President Trump hasn't yet realized that the job of the media is not to support the administration. Instead, it is to provide information and to hold power accountable. In short, the media, at its core, is a counter-balance to political leadership. The E.W. Scripps News Media Company's motto is, "Give light, and the people will find their own way." News media people are devoted to that philosophy.

President Trump has proven to be the P.T. Barnum of politics. Folks, that isn't all bad. There is no doubt that, like the circus that traveled the country for a century and a half, he can gather a crowd and mystify the gathering. No one has done it better in recent years. Our democratic approach to governance gives him three more years to make good things happen for the country using his unique approach. "Hope does spring eternal."

THE CENTER CANNOT HOLD

A friend engaged me in a political discussion earlier this week. He said, "We are overdue for the creation of a third political party." His lament related to his strong feeling that the Republicans, influenced by the Tea Party faction, have been pulled strongly to the right. The Democrats, in contrast, influenced by Senators Elizabeth Warren and Bernie Sanders, have moved strongly to the left. Those who take a moderate center position are left with no party and no leadership.

I was reminded of a William Butler Yeats poem called "The Second Coming," that was written back in 1919 and has often been quoted. Thus, the following:

Things fall apart, the center cannot hold.
More anarchy is loosed upon the world,
The blood-dimmed tide is loosed, and everywhere
The ceremony of innocents is drowned.
The best lack all conviction, while the worst are full of passionate intensity.

If ever there was a time when "the center cannot hold," and "the worst are full of passionate intensity," it is now. We seem to have no middle ground. Everywhere we see the extremes. The "passionate intensity" of radio talk show hosts such as Rush Limbaugh and Glen Beck, both of whom have suggested the use of violence on those with whom we disagree, tell us to act on our most base instincts. Even our President suggested that campaign protesters should be attacked. "That's it, hit him in the face."

When Yeats wrote "The blood-dimmed tide is loosed," could he have envisioned the mayhem that has been unleashed on several elementary schools across the country? Could he have foreseen the tragedy of events in many of our cities?

Congressmen and Senators have been elected after having committed that they would not compromise on political issues. (That, despite the fact that the very definition of politics includes the word, "compromise.") That has led to the least productive Congress in history each of the past three sessions. The answer to why nothing of substance gets through Congress is easy to assess. Those who represent the extremes in political philosophy refuse to compromise to the middle. So, nothing gets done. The result is that the public's rating of congress is the lowest of all time, and with good reason.

So, would a third political party with a middle of the road philosophy win elections? History tells us the answer to that question is, "No." A third party candidate has only won the presidency once in history. Think hard and you will remember who that third party candidate was. In the 1850s the Republican Party was that third political party. It was organized in 1854. Abraham Lincoln won the election of 1860 as a Republican, a third party candidate. No third party candidate has placed closer to the top than third in a presidential race since. Still, if it happened once, it could happen again.

Those who take a moderate center position are left with no party and no leadership.

We are long overdue for "the best" of Yeat's poem to regain their convictions. Our tendency is to refer often to "they" in Washington DC. In truth, the key word is "we". We get who we vote for. Several things should be on the list we use to evaluate a candidate for office but "character" should top that list.

"If we are to survive as a democracy governed by the ballot and not the bullet, we had better act fast to regain our footing. If we don't the "anarchy" foreseen by Yeats in his poem of 1919 will leave us without the moral and political climate to lead the country, much less the world, in the century ahead." The signs tell us we are approaching that precipice.

I am indebted to a friend, John Stringer Rainey (now deceased), for the closing quotation above. He shaped my thinking on this subject with an article he wrote for the South Carolina State Newspaper in February of 2011.

TALKING ABOUT CHARACTER

Webster's dictionary defines character as "the total sum of the distinguishing qualities of a person, group, or thing." We can further define "distinguishing qualities" as those aspects of a person's behavior that tell us not only what he/she has done but what is likely to be done when faced with a moral dilemma in the future.

Can you remember when issues such as a person's religious foundations, demonstrated morality, honesty, integrity, and all aspects of the person's character were evaluated before we put an "X" by a name on an election ballot?

We have been astounded by the front pages of our newspapers in recent weeks as highly respected men in professions from film making and television, to politics have been singled out because of accusations of sexual harassment. One lady, wanting to be anonymous, raised a question on facebook about others who might have been harassed. She was astounded to get back more than 30,000 positive responses almost immediately. It precipitated the national movement now identified as "#Me too," credited to social activist Tarana Burke and Actress Alyssa Milano.

We want people in leadership positions we can trust, who have high standards of morality, integrity, and honesty.

The numbers on that "#Me Too" list take your breath away. Within twenty-four hours the numbers exceeded 4.7 million respondents saying "It happened to me, too." Lest you think these are all just anonymous postings, some of the names on that list are well known including Reese Witherspoon, Sheryl Crow, Patricia Arquette, Viola Davis, Molly Ringwald, and the list goes on and on.

Many of the men singled out as predators are well known too. Bill Cosby of TV sit-com fame leads the list, followed by Harvey Weinstein, Matt Lauer, Al Franken, and a legion of others of both national and political fame. It leaves one to ask the question, "Who is not on the list?"

There is little an individual can do about such harassment in non-political settings. However, we can do something about such people leading our country in our states and in Washington DC. As the title of this column suggests, I am talking about the CHARAC-TER of those we elect to high office.

Many of the basic principles of our government came from the Bible. What does the Bible say about the qualifications for leadership? You can find it in several places but the best and most concise is in 1st Timothy. It tells us to qualify for leadership a person must be trustworthy, above reproach, the husband of one wife, self-controlled, sober-minded, respectable and disciplined. This last trait is further defined as, "having one's emotions, impulses, and desires under control."

The point of this column is that comments such as, "He promised to drain the swamp," and "He is a millionaire, he must be smart," may register as important. Of course, what is important to you may not be as important to me. We are all going to look at political candidates through different windows. However, one requirement that should lead the list for each one of us is personified in the word, "Character."

We want people in leadership positions we can trust, who have high standards of morality, integrity, and honesty, and will always lean on the founding principles of our country. The word is "Character." Put it on your list for the elections of 2018 and 2020.

UP IS DOWN, DOWN IS UP: WHAT NOW?

We have just been through the most unconventional Presidential election campaign capped off by an unprecedented election night that surprised everyone. Even those who predicted a Trump victory, and there were very few, didn't predict this overwhelming outcome. Most of the broadcasters and prognosticators who were on record with their own biases were struggling for words on November 9th.

So what happened? First, give credit to Donald Trump and his campaign team. They read the signs of frustration in the voting public better than the pollsters, better than the media pundits, better than the leadership of the Democrat Party, better even than the leadership of Trumps own Party. When was it that Donald Trump went to the dais in front a political gathering that he did not predict a victory on November eighth? Every time he did it there was this smirk from the media. They viewed it as campaign rhetoric, as just another claim that would not come true.

> **They read the signs of frustration in the voting public better than the pollsters.**

So, what is the media saying today? He ran a great campaign. He read the level of frustration in the American voter better than any of the pollsters. He said the things that hit the nail on the head with first one group of voters and then another, and another.

President elect Trump's opponent was Hillary Clinton but he ran his campaign again Washington DC. There is an old joke that goes, "If you have been in office long enough, you will have made enough tough decisions that aggravate enough of your constituency that they can defeat you at the polls. If you have been in office long enough and you have not made enough of those tough decisions, they will throw you out of office for inactivity." He said the DC leadership had not done enough to solve the major problems facing America in illegal immigration, jobs, international relations, the economy, etc. Those specific problems were not the causes of every American but if you keep citing problems long enough, you will find one that resonates with virtually everyone. In short, enough of the tough decisions have not been made so it was time to "drain the swamp."

How does one explain the overwhelming vote for Donald Trump? First, it was a vote for change. Many people are just tired of the same old, same old. They wanted change. Someone said months ago "We need a rascal in the White House." Many agreed with that statement. Who better to shake things up that Donald Trump? Second, many of the voters were voting AGAINST something rather than FOR something. One lady asked me months ago, "You couldn't vote for Hillary, could you?" She was stating her disdain for Hillary and husband Bill Clinton, painting her with the same bush they painted him with during his scandal marred years in the White House.

My departed mother had a sign in the front window of her house back in 2008. It said in "Pearl Harbor" size headlines, "Stop Hillary." Way too many people believed all the hyperbole in the campaign rhetoric that she was "crooked" and "should be in jail." That, for a lady who, despite being in the public eye for 30 plus years, has never been indicted for anything. It does reinforce what campaign managers have known for years, if you say something over and over people will begin to believe it, whether it is true or not. Need I site the "birther" issue related to President Obama which had no substance at all? Still, statistics say that 30% of our people believed that claim to be true.

So, where to from here? As a friend of mine said earlier, "He may not have been my candidate but he was elected by the majority of the people. He is going to be my president and I will support him." It is incumbent on all of us to do the same. Our democratic way of life depends on it.

WE DON'T KNOW WHAT WE DON'T KNOW

One would have had to stop reading the papers and watching television in order to miss the near violent exchanges that occur across the country every time we approach a national election. Candidates seem to think going "negative" wins elections and, unfortunately, those casting the ballots seem to reward them for that belief.

Two things cause conflict more than any other, change and fear. Change, by its very nature, breeds conflict and the greater the change the greater the conflict. That is also true of fear. When we are afraid, our flight-or-fight instincts get overworked and we tend to square off to fight.

Right now we have had more than a decade of war in the mid-east with a growing casualty list and the very real possibility that we are going to get pulled back into it again. Our economy is making progress trying to get out of the pits but the jobless rolls continue to worry us. The health care bill became law in 2012 but the Republicans continue to run their elections as if repeal is just around the corner. These are just three of the big issues currently in the nation's psyche.

Two things cause conflict more than any other, change and fear.

Just below the surface in all of the conflict is a major concern that has nothing to do with the never-ending health care debate or sending troops to the mid-east. It is the fact that many of our citizens do not understand how our government operates. Evidence of that problem is in some of the shameful comments hurled at our public officials as they attempt to explain the realities of congressional process. Even such national Icons as Senator John McCain, a presidential nominee in 2008, has found himself the focus of a considerable amount of rancor in recent public meetings.

That is an educational issue, folks. Every high school student has a class in Civics where the rudiments of governmental operations are taught. Unfortunately, many have forgotten what they learned and need a primer course. Until we understand our responsibilities and learn how to deal with the ambiguity of free democratic debate, we probably will continue to witness our public officials being abused.

From time to time we are all guilty of not reading and studying the issues enough to be knowledgeable citizens. It is easy for us to think we know something because "we know what we know." What is most difficult to accept is that "we don't know what we don't know." Tip O'Neal, Speaker of the House when Ronald Reagan was president, was asked by a reporter if it bothered him what President Reagan did not know. O'Neal replied, "No, what he doesn't know doesn't bother me. What does bother me is what he knows for sure that just ain't so." To paraphrase Pogo from the comic strips, "We resemble that remark."

WELFARE OR WORKFARE?

President Trump recently called for getting "millions" off of welfare recipients back to work. He also has called for a major effort to deal with the crumbling infrastructure that faces cities and states all across the country. Is it a serious problem?

The city of New Orleans reports that their water pipes are more than 100 years old. This past year, at the end of a rainy ten days, South Carolina closed more than 80 roads, 36 bridges and there were 32 dam failures. Do you remember the I-35 Mississippi River Bridge collapse in Minnesota in 2007 that killed 13 and injured 145? Should I mention the Flint, Michigan water system disaster? These, according to our experts, are just the tip of the iceberg.

Welfare was originally designed to create a hand-UP for people, not a hand-OUT.

Perhaps there is a change in approach with our welfare program that could benefit our problem with infrastructure. What if welfare became workfare? Welfare was originally designed to create a hand-UP for people in difficulty rather than a hand-OUT, which it seems to have become. In 40 years of working with public entities of various purposes, I have never met a person, Democrat or Republican, who wants to give money to able people who refuse to work.

Two decades ago we had 4 million adults on welfare, more than six times the number of 638,000 we have today. With fewer numbers on the welfare rolls it seems an ideal time to go back to something that worked almost a century ago. It is time to recreate workfare, to tie our support for the unemployed to productive work.

During the great depression we had large numbers of men and women out of work and we had major infrastructure problems all across the country. The Federal Government devised a workfare program to provide subsistence aid to families but only when a member of the family would enroll in one of a number of programs that provided productive work. With the administration of Franklin

Delano Roosevelt people went back to work nation-wide through the CCC, the WPA, and several other workfare programs. The Roosevelt Great Depression programs provided no welfare, only workfare.

The stated purpose of the CCC and the WPA was, "to provide one paid job for all families where the breadwinner suffered from long term unemployment." The focus was on work rather than "the dole" because work "promoted self-respect, reinforced the work ethic, and provided skills training and experience."

The CCC program was set up for young men ages 17 – 28 and provided work, subsistence while on the job, and a salary, 90% of which was sent home. During its time from 1933 to 1942 the young men of the CCC planted three billion trees, built lodges and trails in our parks and wilderness areas, and created or improved parks in more than 800 cities nation-wide. The WPA was focused on roads, bridges, and public buildings. Together the two programs employed more than 14 million men and women.

I grew up in a small town in southern Missouri that had a public park, swimming pool, and paved streets all supplied by one or another of these workfare programs.

Today, perhaps more than at any other time in the past sixty years we are in good position to give workfare another try. Our welfare rolls are low and our infrastructure needs are the greatest they have been in many years. Our new president has promised a major thrust into infrastructure renewal with an emphasis on roads and bridges nation-wide.

We are the richest nation in the world with the highest standard of living. We continue to prove that we are not going to let our least fortunate citizens go without food or shelter. The issue for us is welfare or workfare. I vote for workfare. As the popular Michael J. Fox movie told us, you can go, "Back to the Future," and we should.

WHERE TO FROM HERE?

The election is over and all the ballots have been counted. This has been the worst of the worst of presidential campaigns. I have watched every campaign for President since 1948. Being a Missourian when Harry Truman is running will tend to draw you to the radio and newspaper. I would say TVs but we didn't have TVs in rural America in 1948. Believe me, every school child in Missouri was watching our hero, "Give 'em Hell Harry," upset Governor Thomas Dewey, the New York City candidate. That one was noteworthy because it was perhaps the greatest upset in election history, not because of personal attacks on opponents.

However, we have never had a negative campaign like this one in my lifetime. Virtually every demographic group under our flag came in for attack including African-Americans, Hispanics, women, youth, and the college educated, just to name the most obvious.

Today, the challenge is to pull together behind the will of the majority.

We should acknowledge that we never have a campaign where the truth does not suffer on the campaign trail, where candidates are vilified, and charges are hurled about as if they are legal indictments. Even with the constant attacks on President Obama in 2008 and 2012 we did not witness even half of the viciousness of this campaign.

But, today it is over. The TV and Newspapers can move back toward normalcy. We can begin to breathe again. We may even be able to watch a favorite show without constant negative advertisements. However, one thing we need to remember, one important thing is necessary for democracy to work. When the voting is over and the majority has spoken it is incumbent on all of us to add our assent to the will of the majority. Today, it doesn't do us well to remember the rhetoric following the 2008 and 2012 elections when one side swore to "fight the winner tooth and toenail," to "make sure he is a one term President." Those comments were not worthy of

our elected leaders. Today, the challenge is to pull together behind the will of the majority. Remember, when we went into the polling booth last Tuesday to cast our ballot for the candidate of our choice, we were really voting for democracy, for our country, for our future, for our children and grandchildren, for America.

A good friend of mine said months ago, "Well, the devil we know versus the devil we don't." To a certain extent, that seemed to be an accurate statement. That same friend said late last week, "Well, my candidate didn't win but the winner is now my President and I will give my support. We have to remember that we are all in this together. If the new President doesn't succeed we all fail." That is the only attitude those who profess to love democracy, freedom, and the United States of America can take. Anything less is unworthy of us.

2
POLITICS

We live in a political system. That is true of every tribe and nation. Politics is the art and science of getting something done within a group setting. We can see it at work in churches, schools, towns, states, and at the national level. No matter how an individual might try to avoid getting involved in the interactions within society's groups, it is an impossibility. At the very least taxation, which is a part of everyday life, pulls us into the fray.

Today, we have a complicated series of devises that help us solve problems and do things necessary for the public good. Political parties became a part of our national scene shortly after the beginning of our democratic way of government. This, despite warnings from our first president, George Washington, that political parties can be detrimental to a democracy. Still, today most of our changes and improvements at the national and state levels occur through actions by political parties.

At both state and national levels government is designed to operate with two political parties. From time to time a third appears but the primary influence of our government comes from the Democrat and Republican Parties. National elections are held every two years with Presidents elected every four years. It is during those times of campaigning for election that the people have the opportunity to give guidance to the nation's leadership.

Major questions at each of the national elections turn to the national issues that challenge each generation, and each new group of leaders. The leadership presents a proposed set of principles called a platform telling what they believe and the direction they will take the country. The people make a choice and express their will with their vote.

Sometimes the country moves in a more liberal direction and sometimes more conservative. The pendulum swings back and forth with democrats controlling in some years and republicans in others. Over the past seventy years we have had twelve presidents, six republicans and six democrats.

ARE WE FOR TAX CUTS?

Virtually every issue before the U.S. Congress generates a negative argument from some special interest group, except one. It is difficult to find anyone who is against cutting taxes. Having the government taking less from our paychecks, having more money in our pockets to spend, and having a government spending less and moving toward a balanced budget, all sound like really good ideas.

The party in power in Washington DC is hoping to rally the nation with a plan to reduce individual and corporate tax revenue by $1.5 trillion over 10 years. They plan to do this without any corresponding cuts in spending. The reason they think this can be done is because they believe that the tax cut will generate so much economic growth that it will effectively pay for itself. Will it? Can we "cut" ourselves into an economic boom so strong that it will pay for a tax cut of $1.5 trillion dollars?

Can we "cut" ourselves into an economic boom?

Cutting taxes sounds like a really good idea until you evaluate what history teaches us about our economy when we cut taxes as a stimulant. We also have to consider the potential growth of our national debt, already more than twenty-two trillion dollars. Let's see if we can get our economic vocabulary into real English and evaluate the possibilities of this issue.

Are we overtaxed as a nation as compared to other industrial nations? According to statistics from the thirty-five nations who belong to the Organization for Economic Cooperation and Development, the United States ranks thirty-first in taxation as a share of gross domestic product (GDP). Only South Korea, Ireland, Chile, and Mexico levy lower taxes on their citizens than the U.S.

Can tax cuts generate economic prosperity? History remains the best teacher of possible future effects of tax cuts. We have had two significant tax cuts over the past thirty-five years. What happened to the U.S. economy following the tax cuts of the Ronald Reagan and

George W. Bush administrations?

President Ronald Reagan delivered a 25% reduction in individual taxes in 1981 and 1983. By 1990 we were in a year long recession. President George W. Bush created a tax reduction in 2002-2003 and by 2008 we had entered the strongest recession the United States had experienced since the Great Depression. To be fair, both tax cuts stimulated the economy for a while before it began to slide.

Both the Reagan and Bush tax cuts were larger than those projected by the administration this year. In the 1980s and again in the 1990s economic experts predicted that the GDP growth stimulated by the tax cuts would generate only enough tax revenue to replace about one third of the tax revenue lost. By contrast those calling for tax cuts in 2017 predict that an economic boom will totally pay for the tax cuts. History says that will not be the case.

President George H.W. Bush called Reagan's tax cut proposal of 2001, "Voodoo Economics." He was oddly silent when George W. Bush followed Reagan's lead and did the same thing in the year 2001. The sad but true outcome of that set of cuts was to have us in major recession and fighting the potential bankruptcy of several of our largest employers such as General Motors and Chrysler by 2008. Why should we expect more positive results here in 2017-18?

One additional negative of tax cuts on top of tax cuts is that the national debt, now exceeding twenty-two trillion dollars, grows substantially with each tax cut. Sadly, we are leaving our grandchildren to "pay the piper," for our indiscriminate spending.

Our economy is already growing and unemployment is at less than 4.5 percent? History tells us a tax cut will get us in trouble down the line. An old southern saying is appropriate here. "If it ain't broke, don't fix it."

CAN'T WE ALL JUST GET ALONG?

Amy-Jill Levine, an Orthodox Jew and Professor of Religion at Vanderbilt University, opened a recent presentation with the Biblical story of the Prodigal Son using the scripture, "And a certain man had two sons." She then looked out at the audience and said, "Every Jew knows that is a formula for trouble." Everyone laughed. It was a great opening for a speech on human conflict. We could say the same thing about almost any human interaction. Where there are two people, or two groups, involved there is potential for disagreement and trouble. That is true whether it is within families, in government, or business organizations. When people are involved, conflict is inate.

We are currently involved with major conflicts at the highest levels of government in Washington DC. This, despite the fact that we are all one "family" with much to gain by working together. Unfortunately, the far right and the far left cannot see enough merit in the positions of the other perspective to enable either side to bend to the middle so that progress can be made for the government and the country. Granted, it is in the DNA of politics that advocates of different perspectives fight for position and control.

> ... we are all one "family" with much to gain by working together.

The conflict we have is political but, in many respects, it has the outward appearance of a religious conflict. The opposite sides in the conflict, the liberals and the conservatives, believe so strongly in their principles that they cannot give an inch for the good of the country. Because of the polarization of their different perspectives neither side feels they can negotiate their positions without running the risk of compromising their political principles.

The Republicans won the November elections and currently control the House and the Senate as well as the Presidency. In short, they control both the legislative and the executive branches of government and have appointment power to the Supreme Court, the highest court in the Judicial branch of government.

The Democrats see weakness in the inability of the Republican establishment's ability to switch from opposition party mentality to that of a governing party. In short, it seems that everything Republicans try to do runs afoul of the courts or the news media. That seems to motivate the Democrats to resist the governance of the Republican establishment and to give hope for a turn-a-round in the mid-term elections which are still 18 months away.

So, how does one resolve a disagreement where the foundation beliefs of two groups of people place them squarely in a position of conflict? Like Solomon of The Old Testament, shall we threaten to "cut the baby in half"? Shall we, instead, agree to get a couple of champions like the young King David and the giant, Goliath, and let them fight it out to the death? Or, shall we simply be content to let the two groups continue to fight over governmental control and watch our infrastructure, economy, military security, etc. go down the drain? In short, what shall we do about two groups who seem to care more about who is in control than they do about the future of the country?

The secret to dealing with diametrically opposed forces can be found in our management text books and has been used over an over to allow organizations to function in the face of significant conflict. Our President has talked often about applying business principles to government. Here is one place where a good business planning approach would work.

Business management gurus tell us that the secret to continuing to function in the midst of significant disagreement is in three things. These are 1) having both sides committed to finding a solution to the problem to be solved, 2) planning ahead for the resolution of conflict, and 3) focusing on "how" the problems are solved rather than the problems themselves.

Simplistic? Yes. Worth a try? Yes, again.

DEMOCRATS HAVE A HIGH HILL
TO CLIMB IN 2020

It should come as no surprise to anyone when I say that Democrats are in trouble mounting a challenge to President Trump and the Republicans in 2020. The odds are all on the side of the Republicans for a number of reasons.

First, the current effort to cut taxes plays well into a re-election strategy. Having majorities in both houses of Congress, the Republicans have the votes to get tax reform through. History tells us that tax cuts will stimulate the economy for the short term, twelve to eighteen months. If the tax cuts pass in Congress and go into effect in the summer or fall of 2018, the positive effects would most likely run into the election cycle of 2020. We tend to vote for the incumbent when our economy is running well.

Historically, we elect presidents a decade younger than our current president.

A second reason the odds favor the Republicans is that they have a formidable list of possible presidential candidates even if President Trump decides not to run again.

Just a superficial list of well-known Republicans would include Vice President Pence and Speaker of the House, Paul Ryan. It would also include several current cabinet members and, perhaps, one or more of the four Generals clustered around the oval office as advisors to President Trump.

Why wouldn't President Trump run again? The reasons are legion. His experience in the White House has not gone as he anticipated. His campaign promises of repealing Obamacare, building a wall, etc. are proving to be extremely difficult. The popularity polls show him continually below forty percent and not likely to win over those who currently view him negatively. His history is that he doesn't hang on long to a losing proposition. Note the several bankruptcies in his past. When the work isn't going well he cuts his loses and moves on. That is good business and he is, at his core, a business man.

Age is another factor that might persuade President Trump not to run. He will be 74 when the next election rolls around. If he did run for reelection and won he would be 78 before he left the White House. Most weekend golfers have stretched their hobby into five days a week by age 78. Those in our population who are still working in their mid-70s generally need additional money to live on. That isn't President Trump's problem.

Historically, we elect presidents a decade younger than our current President. The average age of a U.S. president at the time he took office is fifty-five. Most were in their fifties (24). The youngest was Theodore Roosevelt (age 42).

Democrats have several nationally known leaders, but none who are in what one might call a "reasonable" age range. By Election Day in 2020, Elizabeth Warren will be 74, Bernie Sanders 79, Nancy Pelosi 80, and Joe Biden, 78. Ronald Reagan was the oldest man we ever elected to the presidency for the first time and he was, by comparison, a youthful 70 when he took office in 1981.

There is another eighteen months before presidential campaigns begin to heat up and someone else may emerge on the national scene who captures the minds and hearts of the electorate.

Being President of the United States is a major "stress" job. President Trump said, "Who knew health care would be so complicated?" Every problem that gets to the White House is complicated. Everything on the President's desk is a gray area problem with multiple constituencies disagreeing on the solution.

President George W. Bush once identified himself as, "the decider." Well, he was. And, so is President Trump. Being the decider is not fun. In fact, virtually every decision a president makes generates enemies who have long memories.

Stay tuned. The next 36 months will be going very interesting.

THE PRESIDENT SAYS,
"GET USED TO WINNING"

Sports are set up as a "zero" sum game. Someone wins and someone loses. Most would agree that Americans like to win. Our whole society seems set up on a competitive matrix. It starts well before Little League age and extends into adulthood and beyond.

A few years back I went to my grandson's T-ball game. What a great concept. Every kid gets to bat every inning. Every child takes his glove and goes onto the playing field while the other team has a turn at bat. Where better to learn the lessons of participation and cooperation. Then someone hit a ball into the outfield and three little boys ran after it like it was one of Grandma's chocolate chip cookies. As the three neared the ball one of the boys pushed the smallest one aside, grabbed the other boy by the arm and swung him into the fence. He then picked up the ball and began running back toward the infield. The runner was circling the bases and several boys yelled for him to throw the ball, but he was not about to share such a hard won prize. Thus, did competitive nature reveal itself in even the most neutral of settings.

Winning at the top levels of politics is not only very difficult, it is hard to measure.

I have loved competition almost form birth. We did not have Little League when I was growing up but that didn't keep all the neighborhood kids from meeting at the closest empty field, placing large rocks out for bases and mimicking the best players of our favorite team, the St. Louis Cardinals.

What followed continued into adult life and only seems to slow slightly as one reaches an older vintage. We tend to admire those who have strong aggressive tendencies. They seem to get things done, much like they used to on the playing field. Competition? Oh yes.

There is a parallel to this in political life. President Trump says we Americans need to get used to winning. He says we are going to win so much it will get boring. Here-in is the beginning of an interesting conflict. In more than 60 years of watching national politics I have observed that winning at the top levels is not only very difficult it is hard to measure. Like in physics, every action seems to have an opposite reaction. When Abraham Lincoln used the Emancipation Proclamation to free the slaves his detractors said it would be the end of us. When Harry Truman integrated the military, when Dwight Eisenhower forced the desegregation of schools, when Lyndon Johnson signed Medicare and Medicaid into existence, when Barak Obama directed the creation of Obamacare, many said each action would be the end of us. Detractors appear each time there is a change in government policy. The point is that criticism comes with each action despite the fact that compromise involves the multiple sides of an issue and is always required to reach a decision at the highest levels. When the critics are after you it is hard to know whether you are winning or losing. Someone said, "When you are up to your rear in alligators it is hard to remember that your purpose is to drain the swamp."

In truth, a president never wins unless the people he is serving win. One could say that winning comes when something good and long lasting is done for the people. The secret of winning is not in coming out on top in the competition it is, instead, related to long term benefit for the people. And, assessing benefits for the people is difficult, sometimes taking decades.

The best advice to our president is to take the emphasis off of winning and place it on long term accomplishments for the people. Then the President can expect the ride to be bumpy but, in the end, the people will appreciated him and history will treat him well.

GIVE TRUMP A CHANCE

The letter to the editor said, "Trump won the election, give him a chance." That is an admonition being repeated all around the country, "Give Trump a chance." It is a request that is worthy of some reflection and response.

Some who were strong supporters of President Obama might respond, "You didn't give our guy much of a chance." Who said, "Our job is to make sure he is a one term president." That was Mitch McConnell, head of the Republican Party in the Senate. Who said, "We intend to fight him tooth and nail on every issue." That was South Carolina Republican Senator Lindsey Graham. Democrats might ask, "Why should we give Trump a chance when the Republicans threw up every hurdle and barrier they could find?" President Obama was President for eight years and they were still fighting him "tooth and nail," right to the end.

Politics seems to rear its ugly head everywhere we turn these days.

One of President Trump's successes is getting his nominee through the Senate and into a seat on the Supreme Court. It is unlikely the Democrats will forget that the Republicans blocked President Obama's nominee to the Supreme Court in his last six months in office. Democrats may remember for many years that this nominee to the Supreme Court was stolen from them by the Republican majority in the Senate.

Yes, I know the nominee to the Supreme Court is supposed to be by-partisan. Considering recent happenings with Court nominees we can shelve that illusion. Politics seems to rear its ugly head everywhere we turn these days.

Can the Republicans cite similar indiscretions on the part of Democrats in past years? No doubt they can. To quote a key line in the stage play, "1776", "Who stinkith the most?" The argument in the play was over who was most guilty in the perpetuation of slavery in the colonies, the ones whose ships transported the slaves, the north, or the ones who bought them, the south. Today in our political parties, as was true in the play, neither side is clean.

One could say accurately that both the Republicans and Democrats are both doing the best they can for their political party. Unfortunately, the self-interest of political parties is not always in the best interest of the country. George Washington warned us about political parties when he left office two centuries ago. He said, "Political parties weaken the government. They create unfounded jealousies among groups and regions." He further stated, "They provide foreign nations and interests access to the government where they can impose their will upon the country." That sounds like it was written just last week instead of more than two hundred years ago.

In reality, it doesn't make any difference who is "right" or who is "wrong." The truth of the matter is that our political parties are not working in the best interest of the country. If the gridlock of the past six years is an indication of the future we are in for a major Constitutional crisis. For our country to be safe and well, government must function. It doesn't have to always be functioning on eight cylinders but it has to function. It hasn't been doing its job and that is serious as per the long term effects on the country.

It is time to put the differences aside. Who will be first to put the country above personal and political self-interest? Compromise is the key word in this mental exercise. You can't define the word "politics" without including the word "compromise." Many of our current members of Congress ran for office promising that they would not compromise. They need to either rethink that position or they need to resign and go home. We can't run a government on stalemate and gridlock. We are well past the time when our leadership should begin to lead in a responsible manner. Should I hold my breath?

HERE TWEET, THERE TWEET,
EVERYWHERE TWEET TWEET

Many seem to be "up-in-the-air" about President Trump's tweets. They say it is not the way a president should communicate with the American people. He counters by saying it is the way a "modern" American president should communicate with his people. President Trump's tweets do not bother me. Yes, I am concerned that he seems to wax vitriolic from time to time and that people in the line of fire tend to get burned with no opportunity to respond. What is of major concern to me is that the president has had only one press conference in his first six months in office. By this time President Obama had six press conferences and President Clinton nine.

President Trump's tweets may show us what is on his mind but they do not provide a positive news outlet for his policies and plans. Without questions from representatives of the press he cannot know what is of concern to

Tweets without press conferences are not a positive innovation of this presidency.

his constituents. Tweets without press conferences are not a positive innovation of this presidency. Presidents need to communicate with the people. With or without tweets, holding press conferences would be an improvement.

We can assume that presidential tweets are an indication of what is of concern to our new president. Since his inauguration President Trump has put 224 tweets into the airwaves. The primary thing on his mind is what he calls fake news. He has focused on the news media for 68, or 27 percent of his tweets. By contrast, the wall, which was a major campaign emphasis has been the focus only 4 percent of the time. Veterans, which were a major part of campaign rhetoric have been the subject of only 4 percent as well. By contrast, President Obama or Obamacare have been mentioned 20 percent of the time. By extraction our president is preoccupied with the news media and former President Obama and Obamacare more than several other key issues that were a part of his campaign.

Beyond the lack of press conferences, my major concern relates to the president's lack of up-to-date knowledge about key issues. In recent statements he said, "We have to make ourselves energy independent," and "We have to get several million people off of welfare and back to work." Both are statements the majority of Americans could agree with. Both, however, would have been accurate and appropriate twenty years ago during President Bill Clinton's administration but not today.

From a factual perspective, we are already energy independent. With the technological advances made in shale oil and natural gas production we are now exporting more than one million gallons of oil a week. We have more oil and natural gas than we need. This brings into question issues such as the mid-western pipeline and drilling for oil off the Atlantic Coast.

"Get millions of people off of welfare and back to work?" Twenty years ago we had more than four million adults on welfare. New regulations plus low (4.6 percent) unemployment have reduced the number of adult welfare recipients to 680,000. It would be good to get all of these back into the job market. However, when the number is less than one million you can't put millions back to work.

Add one other issue to the mix. In public speeches our president has talked about creating millions of jobs by renewing our infrastructure; roads, bridges, water and sewer systems, etc. If we limit immigration and send many low rage earning immigrants home, with our record low unemployment numbers, who will do the work on the infrastructure projects?

The primary concern I am raising has to do with the base knowledge on important issues the president brought with him to the presidency. There is evidence that he has knowledge and information that is guiding his policies and decision making that is based on "facts" that are twenty years old. That, more than tweets, is worth worrying about.

MUSICAL CHAIRS FOR POLITICIANS

The election of Donald Trump as President of The United States created a political, "musical chairs," for politicians. With each change of administration there is a "changing of the guard," in our nation's capital. More than 2000 appointive jobs support the presidency and those are traditionally replaced with members of the new president's political party.

The 2000 jobs in Washington DC is just a drop in the bucket in the total number of jobs that change hands. Many of the jobs filled in Washington DC create openings back home. The state of South Carolina makes a good example. Former South Carolina Governor, Nicky Haley, has become Ambassador to the United Nations, moving former Lt. Governor Henry McMasters into the Office of Governor. State Senator, Kevin Bryant, moved from his Senate seat into the vacant Lt. Governor's role requiring a special election to replace him. Congressman Mick Mulvaney, representing the 5th Congressional District in South Carolina is now the Director of the Office of Management and Budget in Washington DC which opens up a vacancy in the district he has served. A special election will be held in June to replace him.

> **President Trump is filling more than 2000 jobs that will make his new administration effective.**

The same situation is being replayed all over the country as, office by office, new President Trump is filling the more than 2000 appointive jobs that will make his new administration effective. If South Carolina is a good example, for each job filled in Washington three jobs will be occupied by new people back in the home states of those elected or appointed to the vacant positions.

Candidates for elective office have a specific set of requirements in order to meet the criteria to run and hold office at the National level. The same is true back home. Every candidate for office is vetted to make sure they qualify. In some states the vacant offices

are filled by special elections and n others the governor appoints someone to fill the unexpired term.

The desire, as always, is to find a candidate who is best qualified to represent the constituency. If the office is filled by election one assumes that only the voter can know who they believe can best fulfill that role. If the process requires that the governor appoint the replacement for the unexpired term then one can hope that there are not too many months until the next election.

Political musical chairs happen from time to time following national elections, perhaps never more than this year.

PLAN AHEAD

We do not have a centralized plan in place to solve the multiple problems we are facing as a country and that simple fact has us constantly in conflict at the highest levels of government. One might think that Washington DC is a reflection of the state of mind of the country but it is more likely the other way around. Our national leadership is constantly in turmoil. That is reflected in the media and, in turn, it is picked up all across the country.

As a nation we have many very serious problems to solve. These problems are as varied as Energy, Illegal Immigration, Public Education, Infrastructure, National Defense, and Balancing the budget, to name but a few.

Much of the conflict comes as a result of the confusion about the direction our leadership is taking us. The President "Tweets" something and various members of his Cabinet and/or his staff either attempt to explain what he meant or just disagree with what he said. If one adds in the conflicts with various special interest groups and various courts from across the country, our planning/direction dilemma becomes obvious. Congress is awaiting Presidential leadership and they are hearing lots of words but no clear direction. In short, we don't know where the President is leading and whether anyone is following.

> **Much conflict comes as a result of confusion about the direction our leadership is taking us.**

University business management programs tell us that the first item in organizing a business is planning. A well run business develops plans that take it into the future. In the formative stages of the planning process those who share the business responsibilities are asked for ideas so that everyone involved not only has an opportunity for input but, also, will know where the business is headed so they can pitch in to help.

If one wants to borrow money to start a new business and

goes to the bank the first thing the bank will request is a business plan. If a business plan is necessary before a business can borrow money shouldn't our government, our biggest business and the ultimate borrower, be required to have a comprehensive business plan? Our government's lack of planning has the country in debt to one funding source or another for more than 20 trillion dollars. If our people don't know the government's plan to solve the debt problem, how can they become a part of making the plan successful?

Our Energy program stands out as a good example of our ineptness in planning. Because we don't have a comprehensive plan to handle this complex problem we fight over every little issue; the pipeline, where windmills can be put, off-shore drilling, etc. Having a plan would tell us where each one fits into the solution of our energy problems.

Illegal Immigration was a major issue of the political campaign. Our President has promised that a wall will be built. Why? If we block that access to the country we have three other borders that are far more difficult to control than the southern border. We also have an inability to track internationals who have entered the country legally but have over stayed their visas. Solving the Illegal Immigration problem will require a comprehensive approach that far exceeds the complexity of just building a wall. In fact, if we solve some of the problems related to tracking visitors to our country, a wall and the billions it will cost may not be necessary.

Our President has said, "Who knew healthcare would be so difficult?" and "Being President is harder than I thought." As good business men know, everything is much easier if a solid planning process in in place.

Our lack of such planning reminds me of what French film director Nicolas Hulot called the "Titanic Syndrome". Picture a giant luxury ship steaming along at night through icebergs, with all the lights on and the band playing. Picture the results of not planning ahead, of not slowing down and being careful.

PREPARE THREE ENVELOPES

There is an old joke that has lots of truth in it and still provides a smile at the end. See if this one rings a bell.

A new president enters the oval office. Like most on their first day there is some confusion, not only about where everything is but what to do first. After some misdirection the President perseveres and gets things rolling with his new administration. At about the six month mark he runs into trouble and begins to lose control. No matter what, he can't regain his momentum. Finally, in desperation he decides to consult his predecessor, so he calls the former president who is pleased to help him.

After some conversation the former president suggests that he look in the bottom drawer to the far left in his desk. When he opens that drawer he finds three envelopes, numbered one, two, and three. A note attached says, in case of trouble open envelope number one. He opens it and it says, simply, "Blame your predecessor." So he thinks about how best to do that and shortly, every issue, every problem has the same answer, it is caused by something done by his predecessor.

President Trump is not the first president to have difficulty getting his administration moving forward.

That worked for a while. About a year later he was again having major difficulty with the problems of the country so, remembering the envelopes in the lower drawer, he takes out the second envelope, opens it, and finds the word, "Reorganize." So, he calls in his staff, terminates some, and makes new assignments to others. Before long there was confusion about who to approach about their concerns or how to get a hearing for their new ideas.

Like the "blame your predecessor" advice, reorganizing his staff worked pretty well for a while. About a year later there was again great turmoil. Almost at the end of his rope he again remembered the envelopes in the drawer. He thought to himself that the other two bits of advice had gotten him through some difficult times and perhaps there was one more good diversionary tactic left in the third envelope.

When he opened it he sat dejected at his desk for a very long time. There on the desk was the last sheet of paper with the words plainly written, "Prepare three envelopes."

I will let you decide whether or not President Obama left three envelopes in the desk for his successor. Blaming your predecessor and reorganizing the White House staff seem to be remedies already explored in this presidency. One has to wonder what is next.

President Trump is not the first president to have difficulty getting his administration moving forward toward accomplishing the goals set during his campaign. Jimmy Carter had a very difficult first year in office as did Bill Clinton. President Carter never did seem to recover. Clinton, dubbed the come-back kid, was back on his feet and moving forward by the beginning of his second year and won a second term by a significant margin.

Washington pundits have said this is the least productive six month period of any president's administration in modern times. Built on top of the worst "gridlock" years of the U.S. Congress in anyone's memory, one might expect it would be difficult to get the wheels rolling again. So far, the one accomplishment of this new administration, other than reversing some of the Obama Administration's Executive Orders, is placing a new Justice on the Supreme Court.

Of the major campaign promises the possibility of repealing Obamacare failed and is now history. Still sitting in the wings are tax cuts, renewing our infrastructure, building the wall, forcing illegal aliens out of the country, and a series of other less formidable goals. Inauguration Day in January was such a day of possibilities, one laments losing that momentum and hopes it can be rekindled. On that major question the jury is still out.

PUZZLE ME THIS

Yes, I know I stole a key line form the Broadway Musical, The Pirates of Penzance, for this title but it just seemed so appropriate. Over and over I have heard our president and other leaders of our country talk about the need to get our economy going again. It is as if we are still in the throes of the depression of eight years ago. Let's evaluate where we are.

Our GNP is projected at 2.2 percent. In unusually strong years it is over 3.0 percent and during recessions it is generally in minus numbers. Our current projection is not "hot" but it is healthy. Unemployment is registering at less than 4.4 percent, a very low number for us. Economists tell us that 5% unemployment is full employment, with the 5% allowing for technological changes in the workplace.

What are the numbers our leadership are looking at that cause their concern?

We are energy independent due to the development of shale oil technology and are currently exporting 439,000 barrels of oil a day we don't need. Manufacturing set a new record last year. True, we are manufacturing different things than the heavy medal and textile industries used to manufacture. Still, manufacturing is a healthy branch of our economy. The stock market is at a record high and the automobile industry is setting record sales each month. Banks, in trouble eight years ago, reported their best year since the recession of 2008.

The question, "Puzzle me this," relates to the confusion of the national rhetoric versus the reality of the economic statistics. In short, what numbers are our leaders looking at that are shaping their concerns? If the numbers are correct, our economy is thriving. If that is true, are the pundits at the national level "crying wolf" or do they have some "alternate facts," of which the public isn't aware?

Two things continue to concern me and appear to be in conflict with reality. First, the Washington rhetoric says we need to spur the economy with a tax cut. Second we need to limit the number allowed to immigrate to the U.S.

Dealing with the immigration issue first, we need to face the reality of a declining birth rate. The economy is dependent on two things for its health, continuing technological advances and a growing work force.

For generations our scientist and engineers have been more than equal to the necessity to create technological advances. With more than 3000 colleges/universities in the United States we can expect research and development of our economy to continue. However, our country, like most in Europe, has experienced a birth deficit. Our population is not producing as many children as we have deaths each year. Unlike Europe, we have shown modest gains in population which we can credit to immigration. Without immigration, one million or more a year, we can expect our population to decline. Eventually, that will lead to fewer workers and declining economic productivity. Considering that our social security and other aid for the aging are built on workers in the marketplace, that is a serious consideration when we talk about immigration.

Tax cuts sound good to us but lead to recession and growing national debt. The best indicator of the results of tax cuts is history. The Ronald Reagan tax cuts of 1981 and 1983 had us in recession by 1991. The George W. Bush tax cuts of 2001 and 2002 led to recession in 2008, the greatest recession we have had since the Great Depression.

The election of 2016 gave us four major campaign promises. These related to 1) repealing Obamacare, 2) building a southern wall, 3) increasing the number of jobs available, and 4) cutting taxes. In reverse order, we shouldn't cut taxes, the job market is very healthy, the southern wall is a boondoggle, and Obamacare needs remediation but the remedy is, obviously, not total repeal. At least, that is what the majority of our people say.

WHO HOLDS GOVERNMENTAL POWER?

The 2016 elections were noteworthy in a number of ways that go beyond the surprise that occurred when Donald Trump won and Hillary Clinton didn't. I have been searching the history books looking for a time in American history when one political party so dominated the national scene as the Republicans do today.

Perhaps the only time in our history when dominance was so complete was when George Washington won the Presidency pretty well by acclimation in 1788. It was a time before political parties and everyone seemed united behind the General who led our country to victory in the Revolutionary war.

One cannot deny that our country has become more conservative over recent years.

When President Washington was leaving office he wrote a letter to the country. He warned against our having political parties. He said that, "political parties weaken the government. They create unfounded jealousies among groups and regions." He further stated, "they provide foreign nations and interests access to the government where they can impose their will upon the country." Yes, I know that sounds like he wrote his letter just last week, but it was 230 years ago.

The year 1788 was very different than 2017. However, one cannot miss the current situation when the will of political parties seem dominate over the good of the country and we debate on the highest governmental levels the possibility that Russia intervened in our last election enough to have affected the outcome.

For the past 100 plus years our government has operated on a pendulum between more liberal elements and more conservative, between Democrats and Republicans. Conservatives will hold power for a while and then give over to the more liberal. It is the way we have balanced our Supreme Court and have focused on societal change (liberal) for a time before reestablishing the status-quo (conservative).

Both liberal and conservative elements of our government have a role to play and provide a balance between charting new directions and maintaining the "tried and true." Staples of American society today such as 1) desegregation of the military, 2) integration of public schools, 3) Social Security, and 4) Medicare/Medicaid to name but four all became the law of the land during more liberal (Democrat) administrations. Of significance is the fact that laws created during more liberal times stay with us even during times of my conservative leadership which indicates acceptance of those societal changes by conservatives.

One cannot deny that our country has been becoming more and more conservative over the past forty years. Evidence of that trend is obvious when we look back to the mid-1960s when we elected liberals John F. Kennedy and Lyndon Johnson as Presidents and then look today at the grass roots voting strength of the more conservative Republican Party.

So, who holds the power in our country today? The significant statistics follow. The Republicans currently hold:
- 246 out of 435 seats in the house.
- 54 out of 100 seats in the Senate.
- 34 out of 50 Governors of states.
- 5 out of 9 Justices of the Supreme Court were appointed by
- Republican presidents (with one more currently in process.)

This isn't new since Republicans have held the numerical advantage in both houses of Congress and Governors of states for much of the last two decades. The only major change with the last election, and it is significant, is that a Republican is now living in the White House. In short, the Republican Party has been in control of much of the governance of this country for some time, with or without the presidency.

In recent years we have moved from a time of balance between Democrats and Republicans to one of dominance by the Republicans. George Washington would tell us that the country may be in jeopardy because of that dominance. Checks and balances between the parties is good, dominance is not.

WILL PRESIDENT TRUMP TESTIFY BEFORE THE SPECIAL COUNSEL?

For several weeks now the news media has been debating whether President Trump will testify before Special Counsel Robert Muller. He says he will. His lawyers say otherwise.

There is no good answer to the questions that are raised when the Judicial Branch of the government questions the President on possible violations of the law. To refuse may cause a Constitutional crisis. To comply may raise issues that could cripple the Executive Branch for months in the future.

If president Trump doesn't choose to testify, what are his options?

If President Trump is called to testify, must he comply? If he doesn't choose to comply, what are his options? Our legal system gives him two ways to avoid such a confrontation.

First, President Trump may exercise his legal rights under the 5th Amendment of the Bill of rights. That is the clause that guarantees that a person is not required to give evidence that may incriminate him. That law has been on the books since 1789 and is a part of the Bill of Rights attached to the Constitution. It states, in part, as follows:

....that defendants cannot be compelled to become witnesses at their own trials.

However, if President Trump "takes the 5th" to avoid testifying it will cause him no small amount of political back lash. He already is having difficulty working with Congress and such an action may adversely affect any support he has in his own political party.

The second device President Trump might use to avoid testifying is to exercise Executive Privilege. Executive Privilege is not in the Constitution or any of the Amendments. It is, instead, a practice of Presidents based on the necessity to be able to get qualified advice from associates without the threat that they may have to testify before Congress or the courts in the future. By definition Executive

Privilege allows the President to, "withhold information in the public interest."

Has Executive Privilege been invoked in our history? Yes. The first time was in 1792 when President Washington used it regarding his response to a Congressional request for information on an Indian uprising on the Ohio River. He lost his case in the courts. Executive Privilege has been invoked often in our past. Since 1980 it has been used more than 20 times.

Who usually wins when Executive Privilege is invoked? The Supreme Court generally rules against the President, though in isolated cases it has supported the President.

If President Trump decides to invoke Executive Privilege in the current situation with Special Council Muller is he likely to win his case before the Supreme Court? He most likely will not. Perhaps the closest situation to the present one was with President Nixon during the Watergate Hearings. The Supreme Court ruled that he had to turn over the Watergate tapes by an 8-0 ruling. Their written finding was that Executive Privilege did not supersede the need of the Special Counsel to pursue his Constitutional necessities. President Nixon resigned four days later.

Every time Executive Privilege is invoked the President runs the risk of creating a Constitutional crisis pitting one branch of the government against another. The three branches Legislative, Executive, and Judicial are responsible for different aspects of the government but are of equal power as presented in the Constitution. When the Executive Branch of the government refuses to comply with legitimate requests from Congress or the Courts it inhibits those branches from carrying out their Constitutional duties.

What is the likely outcome of this potential conflict? My crystal ball predicts that after a legal battle over the issue, President Trump will testify. Do I predict a "Nixon" solution to the problem? No. It is likely that politics will rear its ugly head and the fact that Republicans hold majorities in both houses of Congress will negate the possibility of impeachment. (Do you think anyone will remember this prediction months from now when this issues comes to a head?)

3

THE ECONOMY

There is probably no aspect of our society more closely watched than our economy. There are more than one hundred economic indicators from which the pundits keep track of where we are, and predict where we are headed. The economy is defined as the production, distribution, or trade and consumption of goods and services by the people. All of us are involved in the economy as both producers and consumers. The relative health of the economy is vitally important to our country and to every individual.

Few who were involved in the 1990s will forget what became the moto of the Bill Clinton political campaign for president, "It's the economy, stupid." History tells us that when the economy is running well we tend to vote for the incumbents in office. When it is not running well we tend to vote for those not in office in hopes a change of leadership will improve things.

Our economic history tell us that since the Great Depression of the 1930s, we have entered a recession on the average of every six to eight years. Those who watch the economy most closely tell us that a recession is necessary in a free economy. It is an adjustment that comes about naturally when the development of technology causes a surge in economic activity that tends to leave a number of work areas behind. Such recessions pass as workers are retrained into the new technology and take on new jobs.

Theorist have shown a relationship between efforts to artificially stimulate the economy and the depth of a recession. One of the ways used to stimulate our economy in the past is to cut taxes in hopes of stimulating more spending. That tactic generally works for a while but the recession that follows is generally deeper and more problematical following such artificial efforts. Good examples of

such were in the Reagan tax cuts of 1982 and the G. W. Bush tax cuts of 1992 and 1993. Both were followed by significant recessions. The economy works better when its wolf and warp is allowed to proceed naturally.

FREE TRADE AGREEMENTS:
GOOD OR BAD FOR US?

Free trade agreements have come under fire in the presidential campaign and it may be the right time to review such agreements and their relative benefits.

The first such agreement that made the headlines was in 1985 between the U.S. and Israel and there have been three more major ones and several minor ones since then. In general the basic theory of a free trade agreement is that if governments, (taxes, duties & tariffs) are not involved the companies involved in international trade will increase their income. In fact, that theory has proven to be correct. The down side is that certain jobs in the U.S. have been eliminated to the benefit of other countries.

Despite the fact that such agreements appear to be politically partisan that is not the case. In past years, such agreements have been sponsored by both Democrat and Republican Presidents.

In past years such agreements have been sponsored by both Demorcrat and Republican Presidents.

The first free trade agreement was during the Clinton (D) administration. A second, called NAFTA, was signed in 1994 by George H.W. Bush (R). The Trade Act of 2001, was during the George W. Bush (R) Administration. The most recent one being debated today is under the Obama Administration (D) and is called the Trans-Pacific Partnership. It is a free trade agreement that includes the U.S., Australia, New Zealand, Chile, Peru, Singapore, Vietnam, and Brunei.

It is true that many jobs have been discontinued in recent years and that is a tragedy for workers who depended on those jobs. The "rust belt" in the Northeast is symbolic of the loss of our steel plants and other "fabrication" industries. The South has felt the economic pressures over the last forty years with the loss of the textile mills that were so much a part of both the economic and social well-being of that region.

It might be a shock to learn that though manufacturing jobs have declined over the past twenty years U.S. manufacturing output has increased by almost 40 percent over that time period. Manufacturing now adds a record 2.4 trillion to the US. Economy annually." Productivity gains created by technology caused about 85 percent of the loss of manufacturing jobs from 2000 to 2010. Free trade agreements accounted for less than 13 percent of the losses.

No amount of political posturing is going to bring manufacturing jobs back to those now defunct industries. If all free trade agreements were wiped out, the primary outcome would be for prices in many of those commodity areas to rise significantly. Not only would that adversely affect our economy but the paying public would be very unhappy with the result.

As in so many other aspects of our society, better education and job training for our people is the answer to lost jobs. Jobs in more technical areas are listed in the want ads every week and continue to go wanting due to not having enough trained personnel in the marketplace.

JOBS, JOBS, JOBS

I was in Missouri attending a reunion a few weeks back and a lady from Sikeston, MO informed me that, "Everyone around there is voting for Trump." I asked her why. She said that, "Since the Noranda Plant closed everyone was out of work and anyone who says they will bring back jobs is going to get their vote."

The Noranda Plant she was referring to was located just south of Sikeston at New Madrid, Mo. It opened in 1968, employed more than 900 workers at its peak, and closed in the spring of 2016. The result is unusually high unemployment in the boot heel region of Southeast Missouri.

Bringing back jobs was a cornerstone of the Donald Trump presidential campaign. He said that the loss of jobs was a result of free trade agreements, poorly negotiated. He said he would renegotiate them and bring back the jobs.

Economists say that full employment in the U.S. is 95 percent employment.

This is just one of the many statements he made that has been debunked by the truth-searchers who deal primarily in statistical facts. We have lost jobs and lots of them. However, those who research our job market tell us that the primary cause of lost jobs is the advance of technology and not free trade agreements.

I would be less than candid if I did not point out that people have lost jobs for generations. That is why economists say that full employment in the U.S. economy is ninety-five percent employment. The experts tell us that five percent of unemployment can be attributed to the fact that technology is always advancing and the job market is always changing. Today, unemployment is listed nationally at 4.9 percent. That is about as good as it gets, folks.

The economy of the 1920s was not the economy of the turn of the century. We did not need to manufacture buggy whips anymore. The economy of the 1920s was not the economy of the 1940s nor of the 1960s. Mercifully, in the 1950s our government recognized the problem and began to create vocational and community colleges. The whole idea of these new type colleges is that they coordinate their teaching/training to jobs already available in the community. How successful they have been is in the statistics. Today, two of three (12 million +) students in higher education are in one or another of these institutions whose programming is tied to the local economy. Am I sorry segments of our population have lost their jobs? I am. Do I see a remedy through vocational and community colleges to solve the dilemma? I do.

So, what if you don't have the money to pay for a semester of a community college. Believe me, if one doesn't have a job and needs one, there are government aid programs that were designed to help. An out of work person has only to visit the financial aid office at the closest vocational or community college and share your situation. They have the programs designed for a changing job market.

It helps that we now have more than 1600 such colleges across the country. States like Florida, California, and Illinois have such a college within 20 miles of every student in the state. Most states now have a college or branches of colleges almost that close. In my working life Ruth and I have lived in Missouri, Iowa, Illinois, and South Carolina. In every town we lived in there was a vocational or community college. Their purpose is to help people get jobs currently available in the community. All an out of work person has to do is say, "Yes" to retraining and the process can begin.

There is certainly reason to lament the passing of jobs in a community. There is also reason to celebrate the foresight of our educational leaders in providing a route to new employment.

TAX REFORM: IS THIS STRIKE THREE?

If we consider the repeal of Obamacare and the immigration issue as strikes one and two, is tax reform President Trump's potential third strike? More to the point, if his proposal doesn't pass what is the future of a Trump administration that has total political dominance including the House, the Senate, and the Executive Branch, but can't get his legislation through governmental channels?

Tax reform is a complicated issue. Let's see if we can examine it in everyday language.

First, let's make a prediction. Will Trump's tax reform plan pass? Not a chance. Will some form of tax reform pass? Most likely. Why not Trump's plan? That will take some explanation.

President Trump says that tax reform will help the middle class and his group of multi-millionaires will not benefit. It simply isn't a true statement. The non-partisan Tax Policy Center reports that about 30 percent of the middle class will see a tax increase under the plan. In contrast, about 80 percent of the plan's benefits would go to the wealthiest 1 percent in our country. Reductions in taxes related to the estate tax, partnerships and limited liability companies, and the alternative minimum tax proposed in the Trump tax reform plan will benefit President Trump and the upper one percent significantly, into the hundreds of millions of dollars.

The Republicans must pass some form of a tax plan before they reach "strike three."

Republicans often refer to the Democratic Party as, "tax and spend democrats" and criticize the national debt when a democrat is in the White House. According to the experts who study our economy, the proposed tax reform plan would most likely balloon the national debt by perhaps as much as 2.4 trillion over a decade. (In case you are trying to write that out, it is eleven zeros.)

President Trump says much of that predicted short-fall in taxes will be alleviated by the stimulus on the economy brought on by lower taxes. He says that reducing taxes by his formula will power charge our economy to above 3 percent growth, thus generating more tax income for the government to make up the loss in revenue. Fortunately, history can speak to us on this issue. Reducing taxes has been tried before as a stimulus to the economy without long-term success. In most cases, after a few years of the lowered taxes our national debt ballooned and we entered a recession that cost us more than the tax reductions created. That certainly was the result with the George W. Bush tax cuts of 2001 and 2002. By 2007 we were headed into the worst recession since the Great Depression of the 1930s. Who said, "Those who cannot remember the past are condemned to repeat it."?

Considering all of the above let's assume the tax plan will fail as it is currently written. Why did I earlier say that some form of tax reform will pass and become law? The answer, simply stated is, "politics." One of the primary criticisms of the Republican Party is that it serves well as an "outside" group criticizing the "in" group but when it is given the reins of government it cannot transform itself into a governing party. The Republicans must pass some form of a tax plan before they reach "strike three." They have been unsuccessful in repealing Obamacare and, despite the continual rhetoric from the White House, it is unlikely that the southern wall will ever be built. Thus, tax reform, the third plank on President Trump's three key promises from the campaign trail must pass in some form or the Republicans may face major problems in the 2018 elections.

Can they do it? Of course, they have majorities in both houses of Congress. However, don't expect it to even vaguely resemble the tax reform plan currently being talked about from the White House. That one will be, "dead on arrival," in Congress.

TRICKLE DOWN OR TRICKLE UP

The newspapers gave us PEARL HARBOR sized headlines telling us that we had a new tax law. In the fine print, it said that the new law would generate a one trillion dollar deficit. It was Everett Dirksen, iconic Senator from Illinois who famously said, "A million here and a million there, and the first thing you know it will run into real money."

Dirksen had other things to say that were quote worthy as well. "I am a man of fixed and unbending principles, the first is to be flexible at all times." It seems that the Republican Party has taken that statement to heart. After years of fighting the deficit, citing the inevitability of economic disaster if the national debt, now at the 20 trillion level, continues to rise, the GOP has capitulated and promoted a major tax cut. Perhaps, as former Vice President Dick Chaney (R) said, "Deficits don't matter." Actually, the full quotation was, "Reagan proved that deficits don't matter. We won the elections of 84 and 88 and the mid-terms in between when the deficit ballooned after the (Reagan) tax cuts." Evidently, his success/failure criteria related not to the economy but to winning elections.

> "A million here and a million there and the first thing you know it will run into real money."
>
> Everett Dirksen

President Reagan was an advocate of "trickle-down" economics. He believed that if you gave tax savings to industries that are run by the wealthy, they would spread the money to their workers. Thus, price increases would be held down, research and development would be enhanced and the total economy would benefit. Did it work in the 1980s? Unfortunately, it worked for a time then brought us a major recession.

In contrast, getting more money to the masses has always fueled the economy. That was true whether it was government efforts during the depression years or in the 1950s when unions were in their heyday demanding higher pay and benefits for their members. In short, the approach some refer to as "trickle-up" has been shown to work over and over in past years.

What has been proven is when you give large numbers of people more money to spend, they spend it. In contrast, if you give more money to those who have large financial reserves, they tend to keep it. The former stimulates the economy, the latter doesn't. As old Casey Stengel, former manager of the New York Yankees, used to say, "You could look it up."

I am a long-time observer of the national scene. Why am I so out of step with the majority of the people on his important issue? The answer is in my natural inclination which is to be an historian. I love history, studied history, and at this age have lived a good bit of it. I have watched the economy boom and tank over the years. We generally have a strong economy for several years and then, on the average, we enter a recession about once a decade. Economists tell us that recession is a natural adjustment made in a capitalistic (free) economy from time to time. I have been watching this wolf and warp for about sixty years now.

When we artificially stimulate the economy as we are currently trying to do, we generally find ourselves in recession a few years later. Seemingly, the harder we try to stimulate the economy the deeper the recession that follows. Our economy works better when the natural business cycles are allowed to ebb and flow as opposed to being artificially stimulated. The highs are not as high but the lows are not as low.

Along with the Pearl Harbor headlines about pending deficits are articles about who won and who lost in the newly minted tax law. The consensus is that the wealthy won and the middle and lower economic classes lost. Considering "winners" and "losers," another Everett Dirksen quotation is appropriate here. "The winners never remember and the losers never forget." For sure, history never forgets.

U.S. ECONOMICS: WILL CUTTING TAXES MAKE AMERICA GREAT AGAIN?

The U.S. Economy is a mess. If I have heard that comment once during the political campaign I have heard it a dozen times, maybe three dozen. In 2008 the stock market was in the 9000 range, unemployment was approaching 8 percent, and we were fighting two wars in the mid-east. In addition, several of our largest industries were facing bankruptcy and key financial institutions were facing insolvency. We were, indeed, facing a serious economic situation. However, today the stock market is in the 18,000 range, unemployment is below 5 percent, and most of our soldiers are home. General Motors and Chrysler are doing fine and the banking industry just celebrated their best financial year since before the Great Recession.

Reducing Taxes will stimulate our economy and help us eliminate the national debt. Both the Bureau of labor Statistics and the Tax Policy Center tell a different story. For the past 60 years whenever tax rates were the highest more jobs were created than when tax rates were lowest. Our highest tax period was from the mid-50s to the early 80s. During that period, the government created the Interstate Highway

I'm sure I am not the only one who believes that American has never stopped being great.

System, made massive investments in education and science, created small-business incubators and built bridges to the rest of the world for trade. The results were 50 years of economy growth and the highest living standard in the world.

Make American Great Again. Surely, I'm not the only one who believes that America has never stopped being great. Let's review the facts and you can correct me if you think I am wrong.

Who created for the world the United Nations that still makes its home in New York City? Note the presence under its umbrella of UNICEF and The World Bank who share benevolent services and money with countries around the globe? Who rebuilt all of Europe and Asia following the great wars?

Anywhere in the world where there is a disaster four out of five aid workers, medical doctors, fire and rescue personnel on the scene working with the people are from the U.S. It always amazes me that wherever the tragedy occurs, within hours it is Americans who suddenly appear with picks and shovels, white coats and stethoscopes, hot food and encouragement. Who leads the world in providing humanitarian aid after earthquakes and hurricanes? Who indeed, the people of the United States of America, that's who, the country build on the great ideal, the country that continues to fall short of its promise but is head and shoulders above every other that ever existed in taking care of the needs of hurting people both here at home and around the world. When the chips are down you can count on Americans.

During the election campaign every time I heard "Make American Great Again," my mind rebelled and said, "Wait a minute, AMERICA HAS NEVER STOPPED BEING GREAT."

WANT TO HELP PRESIDENT TRUMP
SUCCEED? HERE'S HOW.

During the past election campaign I was on the road in the mid-west. Everywhere I went people were talking about the campaign. One lady told me, "Everyone around here is going to vote for Trump. He has promised to bring the jobs back and we have lots of unemployment in this region." Her prediction came true. Her section of Missouri and the entire state voted for Trump. Actually, they voted for jobs. That was also true in the states of Pennsylvania, Michigan, Wisconsin, and Minnesota, the so-called blue wall that virtually always votes for the Democrat candidate. Not so this year. They voted for Trump. They voted for jobs.

More than half of the automobiles sold in the U.S. today are made in other countries.

The national unemployment statistics tell us that fewer of 5 percent of our work force is out of work. The issue in the states listed above is manufacturing jobs that produce products like cars and trucks. The fact that unemployment is down from more than 9 percent seven years ago does not dent the factory worker's psyche, it is the kinds of jobs that is of concern to them. Where are those jobs? Unfortunately, many have disappeared into other countries.

More than half of the automobiles sold in the U.S. today are made in other countries. Toyota of Japan has been the number one auto seller in the world the past several years and currently ranks third in the U.S. General Motors and Ford rank first and second in the U.S. but import car and truck sales totaled more than 9.5 million to less than 8 million for American owned companies in 2015. In short, we rank second in our own country.

Today, international products flood the U.S. marketplace. How could this happen to us? How, indeed. A shopping trip to a clothing store yielded tags from Peru, Indonesia, China, Korea and several more. Shop your favorite stores from Wallmart to Belk, from

Lowe's to Home Depot and see what you can find that says "Made in America". I don't think you will have any better luck than I did finding home grown products.

The southeast sector of the country suffered major job losses between the 1960s and the 1990s. The textile manufacturing base that had been foundational in the economy of the south for eighty years moved overseas. The same thing has happened to our manufacturing sector in the northeast and central sections of the country, the part we now refer to as the "rust belt."

The secret to jobs is manufacturing. Each manufacturing job generates five support jobs. Thus, one manufacturing job lost means six jobs gone. If we buy American products, however, the money stays in America and we create jobs for Americans. Yes, I know it's more complicated than that. Some foreign made cars have American made components and some foreign owned firms manufacture in the U.S. Still, where does the money for management go and who banks the profit? If the answer isn't an American owned company then we are losing jobs and potential profit for U.S. business and industry.

President Trump is going to need all the help he can get if he is to help grow the U.S. economy. Where will that help come from? The answer is "me and thee." And, sadly, if we don't begin to be more discriminating on what we buy, President Trump has no chance at all of succeeding.

Who has the power to create jobs? It isn't the President or Congress. It is the American consumer, you and me. The issue is consumer choice. The more we buy that is "Made in America" the more jobs will be available for our friends and neighbors. Will it cost a bit more. Probably. But, if we are lucky enough to have a job, we shouldn't notice it so much. Check the labels on what you buy. The job you save may be your own.

4

THE 2ND AMENDMENT

A high ranking office of the Russian military was at Clemson University making a speech. In the question and answer period following he was asked, "In your tenure with the Russian military was there ever any discussion of attacking the United States?" He took just a few seconds before responded. He said, "No, such a though never occurred to any of us. We were very much aware that American is a gun culture. There are more than fifty million guns in the hands of the citizens. Even if American was defeated the guerrilla warfare would never end." In his response he was both right and wrong. He was right that the guerrilla warfare would never end. He was wrong about the fifty million guns. There are more than three hundred million guns in the homes of Americans throughout the fifty states.

Perhaps nothing expresses the differences in people more than how we feel about guns. George Washington recommended to Congress that every adult man be required to own a gun so that they would be ready to come to the defense of the country should we be attacked. (At the time we had just defeated the British but they were still close by, up in Canada just a short boat ride down the Hudson River to New York City.

Washington's recommendation was not accepted by Congress. However, When the Constitution was passed by Congress, it was accephted with the promise that additional amendments would be added that would be called the "Bill of Rights." Among these would be a strong statement on the right to own a weapon.

Today, we struggle with the 2nd Amendment, its wording, its meaning and its effect on our society. Deaths from guns in the United States (30,000 +) outstrip deaths by any other cause other than automobile accidents.

Shootings in schools and churches, malls and on the streets, continue to confound the experts. What to do about the carnage continues to escape us.

GUNS DON'T KILL PEOPLE: REALLY?

From time to time I take my life in my own hands and write a column that I know lots of people will not like. This is one of those times.

The headlines in Milwaukee say homicides are up 80%. In Chicago they are up 23%. In Charlotte five more are dead in a drive-by shooting. The United States is on schedule to set a new all-time record of gun deaths in 2015.

I am not a gun person. I have many friends who are gun people, believe everyone should have at least one, and wonder about my sanity when I admit that I don't own one. The fact that more than 30,000 people were killed by guns in this country last year and that a gun in the home is four times as likely to kill a family member as an intruder are statistics we should ponder.

The U.S. is on schedule to set a new all-time record of gun deaths in this year.

Some of our citizens believe that the Second Amendment to the Constitution that guarantees the right to own a gun was written so the population could protect itself against a tyrannical government. I used to teach government so I am very familiar with the Second Amendment and know why it was included by patriot George Mason IV who wrote it and George Washington who strongly supported it. It was so that Americans would be armed and ready to defend our government against potential invaders from the outside. Remember, in 1790 when the Second Amendment was written the British were still just across our northern border in Canada and we didn't have a standing army or even a police force at the time.

Here is an irony. We honor our men and women in the military. Have we considered that if having guns was really for the purpose of protecting ourselves from a tyrannical government just who the enemy would be? Logic should tell us it would be those same men and women we revere, marching under the stars and stripes

with the President as commander in chief.

An American who needs a gun to make war on his government must be contemplating another Civil War. In the 1860s that was brother against brother and neighbor against neighbor and more than 700,000 casualties. At least the Civil War was about real issues and not an imagined threat from our government.

Having a hunting rifle is one thing but no one should be allowed to justify possession of hugely powerful guns that can massacre a crowd of movie goers, mall shoppers, or school children quickly and efficiently because those guns might one day be needed to be turned on our own government.

Guns don't kill people? Really? What are certain kinds of guns but killing machines designed to kill people? Folks, we have to be smarter than this.

MORE ON GUNS AND THE
2ND AMENDMENT

A few months back I wrote a column entitled, "Guns don't kill people. Really?" My column will usually draw between 20 and 30 responses each week, some positive and some negative. The "Guns don't kill people," column kept me answering E-mails through much of the next week and beyond.

For those who believe that I am twisting the tail of the tiger by again broaching the sore subject of the 2nd Amendment and gun control please view this effort as one of promoting discussion. I am not for removing guns from homes. Such would be as impossible as sending 11 million illegal aliens back to their home countries. We have to make the best of our current situation. And, the American people have guns, more than three hundred million of them, and most are not for going deer hunting on the weekend.

The American people have more than three hundred million guns and most are not for going deer hunting on the weekend.

The second Amendment reads as follows, "A well regulated militia, being necessary to the security of a free State, the right of the People to keep and bear arms shall not be infringed."

When the "Guns don't kill people," column was published I heard from a number of NRA members. The NRA has often claimed that back in the late 18th century the men who are known as the "framers" of the U.S. Constitution and the Bill of rights adopted the 2nd Amendment because they wanted an armed population that would have the weaponry at hand to take down the U.S. government should it become tyrannical. The actual history which preceded the 2nd Amendment says otherwise. It says, in fact, that the framers of the constitution wanted a strong federal government. To protect that government, they wanted a 2nd Amendment that would legally create citizen-based militias capable of stopping rebellions and insurrections against state or federal governments.

So, why did the framers of the Constitution believe they needed an armed militia? The key leaders of the United States at the time were wealthy members of what was in effect an American aristocracy, men like George Washington, James Madison, Thomas Jefferson, John Adams, and Benjamin Franklin. Because of their own experience and knowledge of European countries, especially England and France, they clearly understood the need for an orderly, controlled, and smooth-running society, not only for the general population but also to protect their own economic interests. They understood this because they and many other Americans had already experienced the negative effects of citizen rebellions that had taken place both before and after the writing of the Bill of Rights (1791).

Beginning today I am going to write three columns that relate to the "gun" issue of the 2nd Amendment of the Constitution. They will appear over the next couple of months so stay tuned.

THE 2ND AMENDMENT
AND SHAY'S REBELLION

This is the second of three columns in a series that relate to the purpose of the 2nd Amendment and the "gun" issue that continues to fester in our society. The focus in this column is in the feeling of necessity by the country's leadership to have a means to enforce federal law and to protect the government from citizen rebellions.

The 2nd Amendment became the law of the land in 1791. Prior to that Daniel Shays, a former captain in the continental Army, became the leader of a citizen's rebellion that disrupted the state of in Massachusetts. The rebellion was against what Shays and other farmers believed were high taxes. This was two years before the passage of the U.S. Bill of Rights with its all-important 2nd Amendment.

> **The purpose of the 2nd Amendment was to strengthen the federal government against rebellion and insurrection.**

Retired General George Washington was so upset by Shays Rebellion that he wrote three letters commenting on it. Excerpts from these letters follow: "But for God's sake tell me what is the cause of all these commotions. Do they proceed from licentiousness, British influence disseminated by Tories, or real grievances which admit of redress?' In a second letter he worried that, "Commotion of this sort, like snow-balls, gather strength as they roll, if there is no opposition in the way to divide and crumble them." Later he wrote, "If three years ago any person had told me that at this day I should see such a formidable rebellion against the laws and constitutions or our own making as now appears, I should have though him a bedlamite, a fit subject for a mad house."

Shays Rebellion was eventually put down when a group of wealthy merchants in Boston pooled their resources and created their own militia to quell the uprising. In the early 1790s a second

major rebellion began in Western Pennsylvania. It was called the Whisky Rebellion and, again, was a revolt against taxes. The U.S. Congress reacted to this second major rebellion by passing "The Militia Act" which gave teeth to the 2nd Amendment by requiring all military-age "free adults" to stand for service to "enforce the laws of the Union, thereby insuring "domestic tranquility." President Washington himself gave orders to form a militia of 13,000 men to put down the Whisky Rebellion. His words later were ".....this is how a "well-regulated Militia" should be used to serve the government in maintaining a strong "security" in each state. He could have added, "as the 2nd Amendment of The bill of Rights says it should."

From the letters written by George Washington and the actions of Congress it is obvious that the purpose of the 2nd Amendment was to strengthen the Federal Government against rebellion and insurrection. It was not, as some contend, to equip the citizens to make war on the government. Stay tuned for the 3rd column in this series in future weeks.

THE NECESSITY OF THE 2ND AMENDMENT

This is the third of a three part series on the 2nd Amendment and the issue of gun control that continues to fester in our country. It comes on the heels of homegrown tragedies such as Columbine, Sandy Hook, San Bernardino, and Orlando where US. Citizens, whether unbalanced or with criminal intent, took military type weapons and leveled them at our own people, many of them children. To restate a disclaimer from the first column in this series, I am not for removing guns from the homes. That would be as impossible as sending eleven million illegal aliens back to their home countries. Righting some wrongs is just not feasible. We have to make the best of our current situation.

For several years following the Revolutionary War there was no militia anywhere in the country.

The second Amendment reads, "A well regulated militia, being necessary to the security of a free State, the right of the People to keep and bear arms shall not be infringed."

At the end of the Revolutionary War the leadership of the country was not for having a standing army. General George Washington gave his sword to Congress in a symbolic gesture and recommended that the army be disbanded. Still concerned about the British occupying Canada just up the Hudson River from New York City, he suggested that a law be passed that every military-age male be required to have a firearm, so that he could bring his own rifle if called back into service should the British decide to invade the country from the north. That proposed law failed to pass.

It is no coincidence that two of the major issues debated by the delegates to the Constitutional Convention in 1787 were how to best preserve and protect the "tranquility of the Union" and how to allocate more power to the office of the president and federal courts, while at the same time preserving the rights and power of individual states. Almost from the beginning the U.S. has had two major groups with different political philosophies. Those who became known as "Federalists" argued for a strong presidency and a strong central government. The "Anti-Federalists" argued for governing documents that would guarantee strong state's rights. Because of the rebellions already experienced the Anti-Federalists were willing to concede that the Federal government needed more power than it has been given under the Articles of Confederation. Thus, the wording in the new Constitution and the Bill of Rights, with its all-important 2nd Amendment, were designed to strengthen and protect the Federal government.

For several years following the Revolutionary War there was no militia anywhere in the country. Then came the Shays Rebellion in Massachusetts quickly followed by the Whisky Rebellion in Western Pennsylvania. Those citizen uprisings alerted the leadership that something was needed to protect the state and federal government from such threats. It is no coincidence that the 2nd Amendment was written and passed in the midst of the turmoil of the Shays Rebellion and just at the start of the uprising in Pennsylvania.

Note that the Amendment begins with the preface about a "well regulated militia." Had the emphasis of the writer (George Mason IV) been otherwise he would have led with "The right of the people to keep and bear arms shall not be infringed." Instead he chose to emphasize the "militia." By the time the bill of Rights went to the states for ratification in 1791 all were aware of the need for a militia. It passed with little decent.

Resources used for these column came from His Excellency: George Washington by Joseph Ellis (2004), James Madison's arguments for a strong federal government in The Federalist Papers, (1777-78), and The readers Companion to American History by Foner and Garraty, which tells the history of Shays Rebellion and the Whisky Rebellion.

If interested readers missed either of the first two columns in this series, feel free to write me at presnet@presnet.net and request the earlier columns. I will be pleased to send them.

5

EDUCATION

An old farmer from the mid-west was addressing a group. He said, "If you are going to be critical of farmers, don't speak with your mouth full." I might echo that sentiment for teachers and schools. "If you are going to write something critical of our schools and the teachers who are at the soul of every educational endeavor, remember where you learned to write and who taught you."

History tells us that the first schools in the United States were private units like Harvard and William and Mary. These were schools for the elite, the wealthy, the land holders. It was Thomas Jefferson who said, "Educate and inform the whole mass of the people. They are the only sure reliance for the preservation of our liberty." Thus, from the genius mind of Thomas Jefferson came education for the masses, public education.

Thomas Jefferson, himself the son of wealthy land holders, saw the value of education for everyone. He saw it as insurance that our government, a glorious experiment in democracy, was dependent on everyone having an understanding of the world around them. He said, "To penetrate these clouds of darkness, the general mind must be strengthened by education. Wherever the people are well informed they can be trusted with their government."

It may be a bit hard to grasp in this day of "education for the job market," but the primary reason for education in the minds of our founding fathers was to create informed citizens capable of participating in their own government.

Winston Churchill famously said, "The best argument against democracy is a five-minute conversation with the average voter." I can understand that sentiment from Prime Minister Churchill considering that the British system of education has never been designed

to educate the entire population. By the time the masses in England were given the vote, few were capable of exercising that right in an intelligent manner. They simply had not been educated to be citizens.

TEACHER APPRECIATE WEEK: MAY 6-12

Their names were Miss Cooper, Mrs. Smith, Miss Stubbs, Mrs. Williams, Mrs. Jenkins, Mrs. Bailey, Mrs. Leuellen, and Mrs. Hood.

Those names mean nothing to you, but they mean a great deal to me. They are the teachers who, more than 60 years ago, taught the first eight grades in a rural school in Southern Missouri when I was a boy.

Their names, their faces, their spirit and enthusiasm are as vivid in my mind today as the faces of the people I encounter every day. Why, if I can recall their faces so easily can't I recall the faces of my neighbors and my school friends of that time? Why do I remember so vividly those ladies' faces from so many years ago?

Education is largely a product of the relationship between a student and the teacher.

They were my teachers. They were the overworked, under-paid ladies of another age who were dedicated to my well-being, to my development as a person, to my future.

How I would love to see them all again—to tell them that I did learn to spell, to multiply, and where that train headed west from Detroit and the car headed east from Chicago passed each other, that I turned out all right, what they meant to me.

All of us have similar memories. I have called them forward to remind us all that education is largely a product of the relationship between a student and the teacher. That it is, as a former U.S. president said, "…a student on one end of a log and a teacher on the other…" That no matter how many computers or movie projectors we buy for our classrooms, the teacher is still the catalyst that makes the process work. When we talk about more money for education we are talking about more money for teachers and their students. When we talk about improving education we are really talking about improving teaching and the learning environment.

At Anderson University, where I was president for several years, we have an awards mechanism whereby the Alumni Association recognizes an outstanding teacher each year. The mechanism calls for nomination and testimonials to come from students. To read the material provided by students on their teachers is both fascinating and eye opening.

One student wrote about a teacher who bolstered his sagging confidence, another wrote about a teacher's patience, a third about how a teacher inspired her to work harder. The comments were many and varied, a tribute to the teacher's ability to provide for each student just what is needed to motivate that particular student.

Students both need and want to be pushed. They like teachers who extract the most from them, and they profoundly love those who give individual help when they feel stretched to their limit.

The point I am trying to make is this; When one talks about "education" or "school" it is not so much a place as it is a relationship, and that relationship is created primarily by the teacher.

When we think of our schools we must realize the truth of that statement. In the final analysis the teachers, in a very real sense, are the school.

I have known schools that are not as good as their teachers. That can be true if the school lacks resources, it the library or equipment is inadequate, if the learning environment is poor.

But think of this. A school will never be better than its teachers, and the learning environment never better than the teacher creating it. No amount of resources, equipment or physical plant can compensate for a weak teaching staff.

In the final analysis, the whole purpose of the state educational bureaucracy, the statewide taxation mechanism, the local investment of hundreds of millions of both public and private monies in facilities and equipment….. is to get the best teacher possible, with the best preparation possible into a positive learning environment with a group of young people.

DON'T TALK DOWN
TO THE AMERICAN PEOPLE

Please forgive me if I appear a bit frustrated with the level of the political debate going on between the candidates of our two political parties. Much of what is being shared from the platform appears juvenile and more reminiscent of fifth graders fighting over the playground swing set. We are looking for "meat" and are being fed pabulum. It is as if they are speaking down to the American public. And, believe me, the American public doesn't need anyone speaking down to them.

In the early 1980s, an article related to education levels stated that, "Eighty percent of all the people in the history of the world who had a high school level education were alive and in the United States." At the time it was a justifiable statement. Not so, today. We are very much aware that education all over the world has long since caught up with the U.S. at the lower levels.

One place the U.S. does not take a back seat to anyone is in the number of college degrees held by our citizens.

However, one place the U.S. does not take a back seat to anyone is in the number of college degrees held by our citizens. Today, more than 128 million of our people hold degrees beyond the high school diploma. That, in a country of 315 million. The closest country to us in total numbers of degree holders beyond high school in all of Europe is France with 27 million. In fact, if we take Canada, England, Norway, Australia, France, Italy, and Germany the total number of college degree holders in that list of countries does not reach 80 percent of our total.

One comparison worthy of note relates to the number of students currently in college in Germany, one of the key economic engines in Europe. Today, Germany enrolls over 2.4 million students in their 108 universities. By comparison the U.S. has more than 20 million students in 2600+ four year colleges and universities.

Germany enrolls 42 percent of their recent high school graduates while the U.S. number exceeds 65 percent.

How about Russia, China, and India? We just don't know. The comparison numbers are not made available from those major countries. Either they don't know their numbers or they don't choose to share them. What we do know is that technical education is alive and well in China and India, especially engineering and computer related programming. We know that by the number of those nationalities that make up the population in places like Silicone Valley in California and in the Micro-Soft region of Washington State.

In India approximately two thirds of all college students are majoring in some kind of technical education. In Universities like Amity (New Delhi Area) and Bahra (The Punjab) priority study areas are engineering and computer.

If we wonder if the level of our college programming is top quality we should rest assured. Students come from all over the world to take advantage of the graduate level education offered at U.S. universities. Today, we have close to 800,000 international students enrolled in graduate studies across our country. Many of the developing countries have worked hard at creating undergraduate institutions to handle their student populations but they still have limited opportunity for students at the graduate level.

So, what does all of this mean? When we hear the candidates and the pundits on our TV sets talking down to the American public, you can you can take it with a grain of salt. The world is a better educated place today than it was forty years ago. But, we don't have to worry about the world catching up with us in the education level of our population in the near future. So, as the title of this column says, "Don't talk down to the American people." Our population is a very well educated group and their ability to understand the world around them still exceeds most of the population of the world. We can hope the level of discourse to take an upswing as the primary season begins.

HOW TO GRADUATE FROM COLLEGE
AT HALF THE COST

Schools like Stanford, Cal Tech, Princeton, Harvard, and Yale all cost around $60,000 per year for a total of $240,000 over the four year period. Even state universities like Clemson University or Georgia Tech cost $22,000 -$30,000 and more each year for a total exceeding $100,000 before graduation. So, what can a person do? The answer is in utilizing the state higher education system in the way it was intended to function. Virtually all such systems have a ladder approach that leads to graduation. Undergraduate education consists of three to four semesters of general studies, English, math, science, social & behavioral sciences. Because of the similarity of the first two years of study, those courses are interchangeable throughout the state system whether they are offered in a community or technical college or in the largest and most expensive of the state universities.

One can get a very good education wherever you take the courses, or not, as you will.

So, here is your lower cost formula. Stay at home for the first two years and study at your closest low cost college. The course work is virtually the same. Then, transfer to the closest 4-year college to your home that offers what you want to study. If you can live at home, do it. If not, take the dorm room and the lowest numbered meal plan and go home on the weekends. You goal is to hold your total cost for a four year degree to under $50,000. One other tip is worth mentioning. The longer you are out of the regular job market the higher the cost of your education. Shorting your college career by one semester may save as much as $15,000 so consider summer school or on-line classes to save time.

But what about the quality of a degree, a big private university degree over a regional state college degree? All colleges and universities in the United States are supervised by one of six accreditation units such as the Southern Association of Colleges and Universities in Atlanta. The standards for evaluation of instruction at all institutions are the same. Thus, the higher quality of one degree versus another is more perception than reality. It may be more a product of big buildings and whether or not the football team wins than in the quality of instruction and learning. If you want proof you need look no farther than where our Presidents went to college. For every George H.W. Bush and son who attended Yale there is a Ronald Reagan (Eureka, IL) and Richard Nixon (Whitier, CA) who attended small private colleges. President Obama (Columbia, NY) attended an Ivy League college but Lyndon Johnson (Southwest Texas State) and Gerald Ford (University of Michigan) attended state universities.

Education is an individual activity. One can get a very good education wherever you take the courses, or not, as you will.

FIXING AMERICAN EDUCATION: HOW CAN WE IMPROVE OUR EDUCATION SYSTEM?

In these trying times we must be careful to protect the pillars of our democracy. One of the most important of these is education. No one can deny that our education system, from kindergarten to college, has come under much criticism in recent years.

In a recent speech, Secretary of Education Betty DeVos highlighted many of the deficiencies she feels need to be improved. The following list was included in her presentation.

- "Performance of our students in comparison to those in other nations of the world is mediocre. With the highest spending for education in the world, should American students be ranking 23rd in reading, 25th in Science, and 40th in Math?"
- "Seventeen percent of black fourth-graders performed well below average on standardized tests."
- "Federally mandated assessments, federal money and Federal Standards, all originated in Washington, and none solved the problem."
- "Common Core, which imposed performance standards in reading and math is dead. It didn't work."

Secretary DeVos gave us a good look at our deficiencies but took no stand on how best to improve the situation. As should be obvious, identifying the deficiencies does not solve the problem. To solve a problem we need to create a planning mechanism that deals with the primary questions that need to be answered. These include 1) What are the deficiencies that need to be corrected? 2) How can the deficiencies be corrected? And 3) who has the best possibility of correcting the deficiencies?

However, before we get to those questions we need to ascertain who needs to be around the table answering those questions. Input must be solicited from teachers, those who train teachers, administrators, state and federal officials, and last but certainly not least, the students and parents involved in our current educational approach.

We cannot follow the failing pattern used in Congress related to our Health Care program. There, only three months ago 100 Senators went behind closed doors and brought us a plan that had no input from those involved in the nation's health care system. It was never even brought to a vote. A faulty process is doomed to produce a faulty outcome.

So, what should we do first? I raised that question several years ago with a state committee charged with making improvements in a state education system. Comments that came back from committee members were more like knee-jerk reactions. The first said, "We need to get rid of all these bad teachers." A second person said, "We have to stop the wasteful spending."

> "An educated citizenry is a vital requisite for our survival as a free people."
>
> Thomas Jefferson

As a long time school administrator I would be the first proponent of a good teacher evaluation system. However, there are two possible outcomes to a teacher evaluation system: 1) fire the bad teachers, or 2) initiate measures to help teachers improve. I am a strong proponent of the latter. There are many reasons for that. Not the least is that we work hard to attract young people into the teaching profession and we spend much to train them. We shouldn't, as my grandmother used to say, "throw out the baby with the bath water."

Secretary DeVos was right. We spend more money on educating our citizens than any other country in the world. However, Derek Bok, former President of Harvard University said, "If you think education is expensive, try ignorance." The key to the future of American public education is in planning. We need to focus on identifying the issues and solving them. We need to identify our best educational planners and get them together with purpose.

Thomas Jefferson was, perhaps, the strongest proponent of a public school system that educated every citizen. He said, "An educated citizenry is a vital requisite for our survival as a free people."

FIXING AMERICAN EDUCATION:
RESPONSES FROM THE COMMUNITY I

This is the fourth in a series of articles on "Fixing American Education". This was to be the closing segment but, with your indulgence, we will add one additional column next week. The response from our community on how to "fix" the system has been significant. We need another week to do justice to the quality and variety of community responses.

It is hard to find anyone who doesn't believe the education of our young people is important. The problem becomes one of degree and relates to what are we willing to sacrifice today for the future of America tomorrow? The key issue seems to be setting financial priorities.

It is hard to find anyone who doesn't believe the education of our young people is important.

Several legislators are calling for us to go to a four day week in our schools as a cost saving effort. This, when we know that children in many other countries go to school longer each day, more days of the week, and more months of the year than our young people. The discrepancy between our students' "time on task" versus the rest of the industrialized world is too great now. We must hope that "saner" heads prevail when our state legislatures meets this fall.

In past weeks citizens have voiced opinions about what we should do to improve our education system for the future. Here are three of those opinions, with some additional comments.

"Parental involvement is a key component in the education of our young people. Without it students tend to underachieve."

Comments: Parental involvement programs seems an inexpensive approach to significant improvement.

"Elimination of the property tax funding for schools and sub-stituting sales tax revenues was a bad idea that should be repealed. Sales tax revenues are too erratic to be used for school funding."

Comments: Every school leader I talked to agreed.

"Moral and Religious training is significantly lacking in our schools. To improve public education we need to get back to our Christian roots."

Comments: Few would disagree that our young people should be taught morals, ethics, and religious tenants. The first question is, "Whose morals, ethics, and religious tenants?" The second relates to where that responsibility lies, with the schools or the parents. This would make a good future column.

Many books have been written on the subject of improving our national approach to education. Debate goes on constantly in our schools, colleges, and universities all over the country on how to do "it" better. Next week, we will include several more comments from our concerned citizens. Tune in one more time and see what your neighbors have to say.

FIXING AMERICAN EDUCATION:
RESPONSES FROM THE COMMUNITY II

Last week we published three comments by citizens who voiced opinions about what we should do to improve our education system for the future. Here are three more, with some additional comments.

"There are some fine models for education systems that need to be communicated and shared. One example of such is the "Call me Mister" program at Clemson University."

Comments: Call Me Mister is a fine "role model" program for our young people and we need more such programs.

If our educational system is not in fine meddle, it is O.K. to meddle.

"If teachers were let alone to teach, not fill out state or federal forms, there would be considerably more 'time on task' available. The bureaucracy always expects the local district to gather the information but there is no increase in personnel to do this task. So local districts must hire people for this with no new dollars and, thus, the budgets are cut for real teaching. Real teaching is taking care of the needs of the variety of different kinds of students, getting them to learn to think."

Comments: This is a statement written by a middle school teacher from District 5 but it could have been written by almost every teacher in any of the five school districts in our county. State and Federal mandated programs are a major issue with our local schools. One major difference in the teacher's job today and fifty years ago is the amount of non-teaching responsibilities delegated to the teaching staff.

"If our educational system is not in fine meddle, it is O.K. to meddle."

Comments: This was a comment made in response to the column on "political meddling" in our schools. That perspective has merit. However, the point of the column was that our educational system was in relatively good shape in the 60s before the federal government began their meddling. Many say "go back to the basics". One of those basics is that our public schools should be controlled locally where parents and teachers have direct input into the process.

I have spent most of the past 50 years involved in education at one level or another. In the late 50's I began teaching in elementary school, then junior high, high school, and finished my career working with students at the college level. My opinion is that our educational system is not broken, we just need to massage it a bit. As my Mother used to say, "We don't need to throw out the baby with the bath water."

Both the comments and the discussion have been good. We will put this subject to bed today and revisit it from time to time. It is one that will always be pertinent.

FIXING AMERICAN EDUCATION: INCREASING TIME ON TASK

It is hard to open a newspaper today and not find something negative written about the state of education in the U.S. Fifty years ago our students ranked in the top five in most key educational areas as compared with students of other countries. Today they rank somewhere between numbers 18 and 25. One statistical reality is that we have not so much slid backwards as we have, instead, stood still while the rest of the world has continued to change and move forward.

In the mid-1960s much of the rest of the world had copied our educational system. We did it better so our students ranked higher on standardized tests. Since that time we have continued in our mid-20th century pattern while our international competition has made changes in their educational programs that promote higher student achievement levels.

One statistical reality is that we have not so much slid backwards as we have, instead, stood still.

In November of '09 I visited both China and India and talked with education officials about their elementary and secondary education systems. There are a number of differences between their approach and ours. A key one can be identified as "time on task". Chinese junior high and high school students begin their classes at 7:30 A.M. each day and conclude the class portion of their school day at 6:00 P.M. They are allowed an hour for dinner with their families and then report back to their schools for 2 1/2 hours of supervised study. They finally are released to head home at 9:30 P.M. Their schools operate six days a week for 220 days each year. In India they have a similar schedule without the supervised study.

By contrast, our students attend school 5-6 hours each day in a 180 day school year. Students in most of Asia and parts of Europe attend 7-9 hours for more than 200 days and some attend as much as 240 days. The average is two+ additional months of school each year around the globe as opposed to American students.

Why do we teach only 180 days? The answer is in the traditions of an agrarian society where young people were needed at home to pick cotton and take care of the stock. Today, only about 7% of our families live on farms. Our 21st century school schedule is stuck firmly in the 19th century and does not reflect the changes in our economic system. Thus, American students have a "built in" handicap when they are compared to students in other countries who get more instruction and have more time on task in the learning process. As should be obvious, we are letting our competition outwork us.

Next week's column will focus on "Politics" and its effects on our education system.

FIXING AMERICAN EDUCATION: POLITICS

In the mid-1960s American education was still considered among the best in the world. Today, our test scores in math and science rank well down the line as compared to other developed nations. Why? Some significant problems are caused by "political" meddling.

It was 1966 when the first of the massive educational "new broom" programs swept through Congress and landed on our public school system. Since then each new administration that comes to Washington DC seems to feel the need to "fix" public education. The results have not been good.

The most recent approach is a George W. Bush program called "No Child Left Behind". Most educators think that "No Child Left Behind" has left many children behind. A key portion of that program seems to say "Let's reward the teacher when his/her students score well on standardized test". Thus, the teacher is motivated to teach to the test which may develop a nation of really good test takers but not much productivity in more important areas.

Knowing little about automobiles, I should never tell a mechanic how to fix one.

President Obama has some thoughts on how to improve our education system too. For instance, he likes merit pay for teachers which, believe me, will never work. I would love to take a couple of pages and explain why not, but that is a column for another time. I suspect his ideas will show up in Congress eventually and our schools will have yet another "new broom" to deal with. Perhaps you will forgive the sarcasm when I say "Oh good, someone else who never spent a day in a classroom or prepared a lesson plan telling the professionals how to teach our children."

Knowing little about the technical aspects of boats and automobiles, I should never try to tell a mechanic how to fix one. The point

is that the amateurs in Washington DC should leave the education of our children to those who are trained and dedicated to do the job. The educational process is complicated. There is no "one size fits all" in teaching children. Creating a positive learning environment must be done one to one in the classrooms of America not by the politicians in Washington DC.

I am among those who believe it isn't a coincidence that student achievement began to drop at about the same time Congress and the President began to mettle in our education system. As Stan Laurel of the old Laurel & Hardy comedy team used to say, "It's a fine mess you've gotten us into now Ollie".

In a couple of weeks this column will incorporate some of the ideas shared by those who wrote in to participate in the formation of these columns on education. If you haven't shared your ideas, now is the time.

FIXING AMERICAN EDUCATION: TEST SCORES SHOW NOTHING SIGNIFICANT

The latest U.S. public school SAT scores show a six point decline. Get ready for the chorus of complaints about how poor our schools are.

After 40 years of watching the test score dilemma I am convinced it is what my grandmother used to call a "tempest in a tea pot." I am not a big believer in comparative test scores predicting anything of consequence. Some say that our students' test scores show that our schools are poor, our teachers don't teach well, and that we keep pouring good money after bad into our schools. I couldn't disagree more strongly. We do have a test score problem but its foundation is in the very thing that makes us strong as a nation.

President Franklin Delano Roosevelt called our country a melting pot. He was talking about the mixture of "peoples" who came to America from all over the world to create our dynamic population of high spirited, high ability people. It is this melting pot that causes the test score lag. The proof is in some of the new research done by the owner of the SAT test battery, the College Board of Princeton, NJ.

After forty years of watching the test score dilemma I am convinced it is a "tempest in a tea pot."

All would agree that there are differences in the races and national groups that populate the world. One of those differences relates to how students score on formalized tests. A recent College Board publication revealed that there were consistent differences in SAT test scores of descendants of various ethnic and national groups. For instance, Asians taking the test in the U.S. scored an almost identical average score with Asians in China and Singapore. Mexican Americans scored an almost identical score with those who took the test in Mexico. The scores of whites were similar to Europeans and blacks similar to Africans, etc. In short, genetic and family backgrounds seemed to dictate the average scores in almost every case.

Since we are the only "melting pot" in the world, we are the only place where test scores are not homogeneous by national and racial groups. That means the "mix" of students in our schools strongly influences our average scores. Our teachers and school administrators are very much aware that the mix of students in our schools has gone through a radical change since the mid-1960s. Today, more than 50% of U.S. public school students come from immigrant and minority homes. That fact influences the outcome whether we are comparing student SAT test scores state to state or the U.S. is comparing math and science scores with the other industrialized countries.

Of course we should make our schools better. However, we should focus on the needs of students and not on some nebulous test scores.

FIXING AMERICAN EDUCATION: RAISING STUDENT TEST SCORES

Raising student test scores has become a national obsession. Everyone seems to know just what is wrong with our schools and proposed solutions to the many problems seem to come from everywhere. It reminds me of the first time I agreed to umpire a little league baseball game. That is when I came to the realization that every mother sitting down behind third base could call balls and strikes better than I could from behind home plate. With every newspaper article on test scores just watch the fingers begin to point. Everyone knows what the problem is and what, or who, is at fault. Unfortunately, Mark Twain's comment about the weather, "Everyone is talking about it but no one is doing anything about it," also applies to student test scores.

Mark Twain's comment, "Everyone is talking about it but no one is doing anything about it" applies to student test scores.

All of us know the story. The students from Germany, Japan, and other countries we must compete with in productivity in the world marketplace continually rank above us on math and science standardized tests. Further, no matter how much money we throw at the problem and which new broom we use, (ie. No Child Left Behind) our students do not seem to show significant progress. The test scores are not going up.

Logic requires that we examine the factors that make up the U.S. educational plan. These include facilities, supplies and materials, curricula, supervision, teachers, and length of school year and day, (ie. time on task).

If one compared facilities, textbooks, supplies and materials, between U.S. schools and others, who could match us? Who has better or more school facilities than we have? In many countries they meet their classes in a nearby church, in the basement of a police station, or under a tree in the front yard of a teacher's home. You should see the facilities that pass for schools in India and Sri Lanka where my wife and I lived for a time. Who has more up-to-date textbooks or supplies and materials than we do? No one. In these important areas we would rank an undisputed number one.

The same holds true for supervision. We have more principals, curriculum supervisors, personnel handlers, etc. per teacher and per pupil than are available in the schools of any other country. Here too, we rank number one.

How about teachers? Across the U.S. the student-teacher ratio averages around 17-1, with some a little higher and some a bit lower. The ratios are much higher in virtually all other countries. Only England and Germany are close to us with ratios in the mid-20s.

How about teacher preparation? The primary degree for teaching in all current and former U.K. countries such as England, India, South Africa, etc. is a three year bachelor's degree. In much of Asia it is a 2-year degree. One cannot teach in the public schools of the U.S. without at least a bachelors (4-year) degree and almost half of our teachers have master's degrees (5 years of preparation). One local school district reports that approximately one third of their teachers have master's degrees and 20% have qualifications beyond the masters. There is no question that U.S. teachers rank number one in preparation for teaching our young people.

That leaves only one factor, time on task, left to compare and there, unfortunately, the U.S. ranks well down the list of all industrialized nations. Most schools in the U.S. are set up on 180 teaching days. By contrast, Japan has students in school 225 days and Germany 223. (Response from Embassies of Japan and Germany, 9/24/07) Korea matches Japan but most students take additional classes on Saturday running their "time on task" considerably higher. You do the math. Japan, Germany, and Korea all have students in school the equivalent of an additional two months each year as compared to our young people. Forty additional days of instruction for twelve years computes out to two full years of instruction more than our students receive. Why shouldn't their test scores be higher?

My wife and I lived in three states, Iowa, Illinois, and South Carolina, while our three children were growing up. Iowa students continually rank in the top three in the country on SAT scores. By contrast, South Carolina usually is near the bottom. Illinois is generally about half way in between. When one compares the length of the school year in the three states there is little difference. However, the length of the school day in Iowa is seven hours. In South Carolina it is 6 ½ hours. Thirty minutes each day doesn't seem like much but it constitutes an additional 7% of instruction time for Iowa students and, over twelve years it is approximately 1080 instructional hours which is the equivalent of almost a full year of going to school. Is it any wonder that Iowa students tend to score approximately 80 points (9%) higher on the SAT exam each year?

Is solving our student productivity problem and getting test scores headed upward as simple as increasing "time on task"?

Is solving our student productivity problem and getting test scores headed upward as simple as increasing "time on task"? Can it be that easy? Lets hope it is. That would mean we don't have to build more schools, hire more teachers, or buy more text books. We just need to give our well trained highly motivated teachers more time with their students. If we want to match Iowa we need to lengthen our school day. If we want to match Germany and Japan we will need to add an additional two months to our school year. Any production line supervisor at a factory could have told us the key is "more time on task"

6

RELIGION

Certainly nothing is more personal than a person's religious foundations. A person's beliefs grow out of a multiplicity of personal history and background. The United States has a religious population. In a recent poll, 89 percent said they believe in a supreme being, a God over all. Our congress that has five hundred and thirty five Senators and Congressmen and virtually one hundred percent positive response to a query about church/religious affiliation.

Once past the mass agreement in a supreme being, the unanimity stops. Much has changed for that time in history before the Reformation when there was one primary Christian religion and its name, Catholic, means "universal." When that particular sector of Christianity was named it was, in fact, universal. However, today that is definitely not the case.

One can easily name what we often refer to as the "mainline" churches represented in the United States. These would include Catholic, Baptist, Methodist, Presbyterian, Episcopal, and Jewish. However, the book of religions records more than 480 different religious groups and confesses in the preface that there are many more that are not included in the book.

When Roger Williams founded the first Baptist church in the new world in Providence, Rhode Island in 1638, he knew for sure there was only one Baptist church and one denomination of Baptist in the new world. Today, there are more than 350 different denominations of protestant churches in the U.S. who use the name, Baptist. Thus, we can say for certain that there are many different types of Christianity, many people with different beliefs and all acknowledge a supreme being.

UNDERSTANDING RELIGIOUS PREJUDICE

A few weeks back a man at a Donald Trump rally called President Obama a Muslim, described Muslims as "a problem in this country," and suggested it was time to "get rid of them." Candidate Trump, who received some criticism in the press for not defending President Obama, stated that he was "not morally obligated to defend President Obama."

At a later interview Presidential Candidate Ben Carson stated that the next president should be, "sworn in on a Bible and not a Quran." (He later said he was misquoted.)

Those are not the first comments insinuating that our president is a Muslim. In the bitter election of 1800 no less a national icon than John Adams suggested that Thomas Jefferson might be a Muslim. The exact quotation was, "...that no one seems to know whether Mr. Jefferson believes in a heathen mythology or in the Quran."

We can be pleased that every member of Congress identifies some religious group with which they have affiliation. We may not agree with their choice in some cases but it is good know where they get their moral guidance.

I am reminded of an old Groucho Marx saying that, "I would not want to belong to any organization that would have me as a member."

It is sad to say but the truth is that religious prejudice has always been lying just below the surface in our society and it bubbles up every time we have an election. Throughout U.S. history, some Protestants have denounced Catholics as fake Christians. Mormons have been targeted with a variety of negatives that resulted in their leaders being sued, jailed, and even murdered. The Mormon people were run out of one state after another until they finally settled in a far western territory that today we call Utah. Can you remember the picture on the cover of a Life Magazine that came from the 1920s?

It was of the door of a tavern with a sign that said, "No dogs or Irish allowed." The picture of prejudice is not pretty whether it is in others or in ourselves.

There is an irony in that the Puritans who came to this country to escape the religious prejudice of Europe became to others what they had hated in the old country. Because of that many moved out of Massachusetts and settled in other places where they could worship as they chose. Roger Williams, credited with starting the first Baptist Church in this country, was one of those. He began his ministry in Massachusetts but started his church in Providence, Rhode Island. A second irony related to Williams is that shortly after he started that church he left it in a dispute. I am reminded of that old Groucho Marx tongue-in-cheek comment that stated, "I wouldn't want to be a part of any organization that would have me as a member."

We all have prejudices. The milder term is "bias". But, even the word bias in the dictionary uses the term prejudice to define it. Having biases is a part of being human. It comes from not only how we were raised but where. It is created by both our own experiences and those of others close to us. The important factor is that we realize these biases are a part of us and that we not let them dictate our behavior towards others. What we believe does affect us in our relationships with others and will certainly help shape our thinking at election time.

Our founding fathers considered several models of governance including making this nation a theocracy similar to several in Europe or creating a protestant nation that would involve a religious test for entry. (Several of our early states were identified as havens for one religious group or another including Pennsylvania for the Quakers, Massachusetts for the Puritans, and Rhode Island for the Baptists.)

Our founding fathers wisely decided on a Constitution that honored no religious group over another and created a key Amendment to the Constitution that spoke specifically to religion and its absence from our governmental process. History has shown how wise they were.

RELIGION AND POLITICS
IN THE 21ST CENTURY

Americans, to their credit, have proven to have a high degree of tolerance when it comes to religious beliefs. We are well past the time when anti-Catholic sentiments cost Al Smith the Presidency in 1928. John F. Kennedy broke the "Catholic" barrier in 1960. Mark Rozell, a professor at George Mason University in Virginia says "This is a deeply religious nation by many standards. People want their leaders to be believers. They want them to have a moral framework as they lead the country."

But, the issue with many may be where the moral framework comes from and what its foundations are. Can we accept a political leader who believes in the Old Testament but not the New? How about one who believes in the Old and New Testament but, also, the Book of Mormon?

> **Our citizens want our leaders to have a moral framework as they lead the country.**

A recent poll from the Pew Research Center tells us the religious affiliations of those who currently represent us in Congress. There are just two non-Christian Republicans in the new Congress, New York Rep. Lee Zeldin and Tennessee Republican David Kustoff. Both are Jewish. Thus, 291 out of 293 congressional Republicans identify as Christian.

There is slightly more religious diversity on the Democratic side of the aisle, though Democrats still are 80 percent Christian. Out of 242 Democrats there are 28 Jews, three Buddhists, three Hindus, two Muslims and one Unitarian Universalist.

The number of Christians in Congress is a higher percentage (90%) than the number of Americans who identify as Christian (77%).

Most of us can remember when a group calling itself the Moral Majority attempted to influence national elections in the 1970s, 80s, and 90s. They told us it was our religious obligation not only to vote but to actively support candidates who "believe as we do". Those quotes are there for emphasis. Most church members, even Pastors, are still struggling with their own beliefs. Most can agree that there are "truths" but finding them is a journey. In issues related to religion there is no "what we believe", only "what I believe".

The point to consider is that The Moral Majority was not capable of deciding who any person should vote for nor which issues were most important to any individual. In America we like to talk about individuality and there is nothing more "individual" than our religious beliefs, other than, perhaps, who we vote for. In truth, the vast majority of Americans care less about Church affiliation and more about whether the candidate believes in God and how that affects his/her moral framework.

It is hard to tell how the religious foundations of previous presidents have benefited them and us as they pursued their responsibilities. In one of Henry Kissinger's books he tells of Richard Nixon on his knees praying late at night in the White House after impeachment charges had been filed. Jimmy Carter, perhaps the most celebrated "born again" President, found it very difficult to make the wheels of government work while inflation hand-cuffed the country. Bill Clinton, like Carter a Southern Baptist, had his own notorious problems.

Having a moral compass is important no matter what the endeavor. But, Thomas Jefferson was very much the visionary when he wrote the foundation statement for separation of church and state. He saw what happened in Europe when religion and government were entwined and we see, today, what is happening in the mid-east. Roger Williams, the founder of the first Baptist Church in this hemisphere said, "When politics and religion mix, religion is always subverted to the purposes of politics". That can't be good.

It is good to think about the moral and religious foundations of those who are our leaders in Washington DC, as well as our own. However, I hope we are way past thinking, "If a person doesn't worship like I do, he/she can't represent us in Washington DC.

RELIGION AND UNDERSTANDING

In a recent speech President Obama said, "America is no longer a Christian nation, at least not just." Several news reporters jumped on the first half of that comment to report that our President said we weren't "Christian". Obviously, that was not the whole story.

As a beginning point, we might need to ask ourselves if a nation can be "Christian" or if, instead, that is an individual matter. A recent poll revealed that America is one of the most religious countries in the world with 87% of the people saying they believe in a Supreme Being. America is also one of the most religiously diverse countries in the world with many different religions being practiced within our borders.

I taught Comparative Religion many years ago. As is often the case for teachers, teaching the course was an education for me. When you look at the five major religions of the world from an academician's perspective you find there are many similarities between the major religions. All teach a moral and ethical approach to dealing with others. All except Buddhism acknowledge a supreme power that controls our environment. Christianity, Judaism, and Islam acknowledge one God over all while Hinduism has many Gods. Buddhism, by contrast, says there is no supreme being.

We should ask ourselves if a nation can be Christian or if that is an individual matter.

Years ago when I began to travel to other parts of the world, having taught the Comparative Religion course prepared me to interact with people of other religions in a more affirmative way. Obviously, I did not know as much about their religion as they did but knowing the basics helped significantly.

Today, the primary partners I work with internationally practice many different religions. In Korea I have Jin Song Kim who is a devout Buddhist. In Central India there is Mohammad Abid who is Muslim, In Northern India there is Rajesh Aria who is Hindu. Each

has been an experience in relationship development. The fact that I am a Christian is a fascination to many with whom I work and the religious conversations are always enlightening as well as searching.

Religious beliefs are a major influence on our day to day decisions as well as our relationships with others. Considering that world peace is at stake in our interactions with other races, creeds, and religions, shouldn't we educate ourselves and our children on their core beliefs? Teaching comparative religion in our schools is not a violation of the doctrine of Separation of Church and State.

We might like everyone to believe as we do, but the first goal must be for all to understand the similarities and tolerate the differences between the various groups contending for their place in the world. Our future depends on it.

WITNESSING IN ANOTHER WORLD

I work for a consulting service called The Presidents' Network, PresNet for short. Over the years we have set up offices in several countries around the world. When the consulting service takes me to South Korea I am always hosted by Jin Song Kim, the CEO of PresNet-Korea. Jin is a devout Buddhist.

Buddhism has been the traditional religion in South Korea but in recent times Christianity has surpassed it as the religion practiced by more of the people than any other. Today approximately 32 percent of the population are Christian while the Buddhist numbers have slipped to 27 percent.

On a recent trip to Korea Jin Song Kim asked if I would like to accompany him on a visit to the Nungen Sunwon Temple where he attended each week. We arrived mid-afternoon, toured the Temple and arrived in the office area where he had made an appointment with the administrative monk, The Venerable Ji-Kwang.

Nugen Sunwon Temple is the largest in South Korea and maybe in the world with more than 250,000 members and well over 300 monks to serve the needs of their parishioners. The Venerable Ji-Kwang organized this Temple in the early 1980s and since that time has become one of the Buddhism's best known international personalities. In the late 1990s he taught Buddhism at Harvard University in the United States.

Our conversation was rambling and covered many subjects. He was pleased to know that I am a Christian Minister and he recalled his days as a Catholic boy before converting to Buddhism. He talked about living in exile in a Buddhist monastery in the mountains of North Korea. That occurred when something he wrote about the government for a local newspaper put him on President Park's list to be arrested as a dissident. Mostly he wanted to talk about the similarities between Buddhism and Christianity, the commitment to benevolent activities in the community, the tolerance for other religious beliefs. As the discussion grew deeper into his beliefs structure I was thankful that I had taught comparative religion at a small mid-western college years ago and knew something of Buddhism, its origins and beliefs.

It was more than two hours later when Jin Song Kim and I left the Temple. My friend had taken us to the office for a courtesy five minute visit and was amazed at the reception and the depth of the conversation. As we were leaving, the Venerable Ji-Kwang invited us to attend the morning worship service the next day. I was pleased to be invited and accepted right away.

It was just a few minutes before nine o'clock in the morning when Jin Song Kim and I entered the Temple. The auditorium which seated more than 3000 was full including people sitting on small blankets on the floor. We found seats in the first row of the balcony where we could see the entire sanctuary. The staging area at the front of the room was resplendent in red and gold colors. There were three huge statues of Buddha and reflections bounced off of the staging area like spotlights were moving slowly across them. Activities were already moving forward with a choir singing off to the left of the stage. The music and the entire service was in Korean so I didn't understand a word, but some of what I saw as very familiar. There was a worship leader at the front, the choir to the left, an order of service that included a soloist and a collection was taken from the congregation.

> Mostly he wanted to talk about the similarities between Christianity and Buddhism.

When the Venerable Ji-Kwang entered the sanctuary the place became instantly quiet and everyone in the Temple stood up. The diminutive monk was dressed in a gray robe with purple trim, very much an underwhelming garment compared to the bright colors and lights behind him. He began to deliver a sermon. After a few minutes I became aware that a young man had appeared to my left. He leaned over and said something to me in Korean. Of course, I didn't understand what he was saying so I leaned back and he said the same thing to Jin. Then the young man turned and left.

It was a few seconds before Jin leaned over to tell me what the young man said. Jin seemed almost in shock. He said, "The Venerable Ji-Kwang would like for you to come to the front of the sanctuary and address the congregation." Like Jin, I went into shock too.

We made our way down from the balcony and down the left side of the sanctuary. Jin was whispering at my shoulder every step of the way. He was telling me what to say and what to avoid saying. The anxiety in his voice was unmistakable. This was his Temple and these were his people. Though we had been friends for several years he had not seen me in front of a congregation. Of course, I had never been in front of a congregation like this, a congregation from another culture, another religion, and another language. I had spoken to groups before where I needed a translator but never to 3000 people and, for sure, never to a Buddhist worship gathering.

Jin continued to mutter under his breath until I leaned over to him and said the obvious, "Jin, relax. You will be translating for me. If I say the wrong thing you can straighten it out for me." With that he seemed to be more at ease.

When we reached the corner of the stage I could tell that the Venerable Ji-Kwang was introducing us. Then the monk walked over to us and handed each of us a microphone. I asked him what he wanted me to talk about and he smiled and said I should share with the congregation the thoughts we had discussed the previous afternoon about the similarities between Buddhism and Christianity. With those words Jin and I were on.

As I was walking out to talk my place at the lectern I had a sudden inspiration. As I stood in front of the huge throng I put my hands together in a praying position and bowed to the group in that ancient gesture of respect unique to all Asian cultures. As I was straightening up I heard a rustling sound coming from all over the sanctuary. When I opened my eyes every one in the sanctuary was standing and then, as if on a signal, they all bowed to me. As they straightened up from the bow they began to applaud. I knew at that moment that no matter what I said in the next few minutes the presentation had been a success.

My presentation did exactly what a good speech manual recommends, "Start with what your audience knows." Buddhism does not believe in a supreme being, an almighty God who controls the universe, but they do believe in a "Spirit" that is inside everyone. That is where I started, with the Holly Spirit that God puts inside all of his children. That was a major commonality. Then I talked about the devotion to our fellow man, to benevolences in the community, that everyone is his brother's keeper, all are beliefs shared between Christianity and Buddhism. It was interesting to watch the eyes of the people as they moved from me over to Jin when he translated, then back to me for the next comment. He was several yards to my right and the heads moving and eyes following the discussion looked more like those watching a tennis match than listening to a preacher.

All too soon it was over. The Venerable Ji-Kwang shook my hand as I left the stage and asked us to meet him in his office in about fifteen minutes. When he came in he was carrying a manila envelope which he handed to me. He thanked us for coming and shared his last words with us. He said, "The folder contains pictures of you addressing our people. You should keep the pictures as a remembrance of a time that has no precedence. I'm sure that in 1500 years of Buddhist history no Christian minister has ever preached to a Buddhist congregation." He smiled, shook my hand and one of those once-in-a-lifetime experiences was over.

The vision of that congregation still comes to mind from time to time and when it does I can't help but smile. I'm sure The Venerable Ji-Kwang thought about giving us some warning for what he had planned but rejected it in the interest of keeping it spontaneous. He was a person who could see the best in his chosen religion and remember the best of the Christianity of his youth. He was also a Buddhist leader with a sense of history. Those evidently came together for him in the rambling conversation of that Saturday afternoon which turned into my experience of a lifetime on Sunday morning. In Matthew 22:14 it says, "Many are called but few are chosen." God had called me many years before. On that morning in Seoul Korea I definitely felt among the chosen.

PEACE THROUGH RELIGIOUS UNDERSTANDING

None of us who have spent our lives involved in a search for God have any doubt as to the importance of religion in everyday life. Religion is important all around the globe and because it is we need to study and understand the various forms of religion, faiths other than our own, and the importance of these various faiths for promoting understanding, friendships, and, ultimately, world peace.

There are more than 400 identifiable religions practiced in the world today. Five of these are generally referred to us as "major" because of the importance of the religion in history and the number of devotees who practice the tenets of these five religions. The five are, in order of their origin in the world; Hinduism, Judaism, Christianity, Buddhism, and Islam. Hinduism and Buddhism both had their start in south Asia in the northern part of present day India. Judaism, Christianity, and Islam all came from a common seed in western Asia in the present day country of Israel.

> **There are more than 400 identifiable religions practiced in the world today.**

Many of us have friendships that have formed across religious lines among people of many faiths. Indeed, in a family business that serves an international clientele we have partners in Asia who are Buddhist, Hindu, Muslim, and Jewish, as well as Christian. Religious discussions are a usual part of our relationship with them. These relationships should help us deepen our faith since people who do not believe as we do prod us into a closer examination of the tenets of our own faith. The more we understand about their faiths the more we understand our own.

We human beings are, fundamentally, religious creatures. Our response to our religious impulse is either to worship God or to worship something that is less than God. As Christian author C.S. Lewis observed; "What Satan put into the head of our remote ancestors was the idea that they could be like gods, could set up on their own as if they had created themselves, be their own master, invent some sort of happiness for themselves outside God, apart from God. And, out of that hopeless attempt has come nearly all that we can identify as the foundations of human misery----money, poverty, ambition, war, prostitution, classes, empires, slavery—the long terrible story of man trying to find something other than God which will make him happy."

At our best, however, we worship God, the Supreme Being. It is the same on remote mountain peaks and broad prairies, in jungles and deserts, in rural outposts and in the midst of our largest cities, humans worship the divine. And, despite the variety of their geographical beginnings and the diversity of their followers, different religions all have certain essential elements in common.

Whether Hindu or Christian, Buddhist, Muslim or Jew, it is our religion that gives us direction, a sense of self-worth, and a feeling of oneness with the universe. It is our faith that undergirds our morality. Our religious beliefs prompt us to acts of genuine altruism. People of every religious group abandon the comforts of home and family and travel great distances to meet the needs of those less fortunate. Through the financial contributions of the faithful, the hungry are fed, the homeless are housed, and the naked are clothed. The imperatives of religious belief send men and women all over the world to minister to those in need.

One of the common sayings in all religions is, "Prayer changes things." For the believer prayer has power to alter physical circumstance. Studies show that people who pray, and are prayed for, experience better medical outcomes than those who do not pray and for whom no prayers are offered.

No religion teaches that it is good to steal, to murder, or to be vicious. Violence and war are aberrations of our faiths, yet each faith's tradition has the capacity for destruction. Christians have been a part of the crusades, slavery, the holocaust, apartheid, and the Klu Klux Klan. Hindus were responsible for the bloody expulsion of Muslims to Pakistan at the time of partition in 1947. Jews raze the homes of Palestinians and mount raids on refugee camps. Muslims waged holy wars into Byzantium, Persia, North Africa, and Spain and some Muslims strap munitions to their bodies and become suicide bombers.

All faiths have the potential to create saints and breed fanatics. Hinduism brought us the wisdom of Gandhi and the madness of his assassin. Buddhism has shown us the tranquil face of the Dalai Lama in Tibet and the brutality of Pol Pot in Cambodia. Judaism has given us the courage of young Anne Frank and the insanity of fundamentalist Baruch Goldstein. Christianity was the religion of Mother Theresa and of Adolf Hitler. Islam was the faith of the poet Rumi and the terrorist Osama bin Laden.

Yet it is also within each faith that the paths to redemption lie. It was Christianity that sustained America's slaves and motivated her abolitionists. The oppressed under South Africa's apartheid were sustained by their Christian faith and it was Christians, Muslims, and Jews who came together to become the leaders of the anti-apartheid struggle. It was men and women of all faiths who had the courage to oppose the Nazi holocaust.

Each religion offers a path to God. We can benefit by hearing what members of other faiths have to say about their seeking God. In their exploration we may find the keys to doors heretofore closed against us. Contrary to our own scripture, Christians have been quick to dismiss the notion that other faiths have any insights into truth and have been content to remain ignorant of the beliefs of other religions. Yet the God who created us is bigger than any single religion. The paths to the knowledge of God may be many more than we can imagine. God is too big to fit into our box.

In our minds we are the center of the universe. Yet, poverty, war, injustice, and oppression are born from human self-centeredness. In the world of yesterday, today, and tomorrow human beings are not the center of the universe. God is.

Religion is the hope of the world for peace because each religion forces us to look beyond our own personal wants and needs, beyond our local or national aspirations to the service of a God who

is greater than we are. All the major religions look forward to a time when all creation is reunited with the divine. All look forward to a time when goodness will prevail over evil; when hope will overcome fear; when light will banish the darkness; when joy will dry every tear; when justice will be as a flood to drown injustice and oppression, and God, the Supreme, will, indeed, be the great I Am.

With thanks to Bishop Tutu of South Africa for an article that helped shape my thinking on this essay.

7

HISTORY

Perhaps the most famous saying about history is, "Those who don't study history are doomed to repeat it." Certainly there are lessons to be learned from the study of history. Still, we often find ourselves feeling like we are right back where we started.

It seems that the world has been at war since the beginning of time. Just in the past century we can list WWI, WWII, Korea, Viet Nam, and more recently Iraq and Afghanistan.

We know from our experience of the past thirty years that cutting taxes to stimulate the economy is a bad idea. It works for a time and then is followed with a recession that erases all of the good that might have been accomplished during the time of economic progress. Yet, here we are in 2018 and, here we go again.

Benjamin Franklin said, "The definition of insanity is doing the same thing the same way and expecting different results."

I love history. I studied it in college, taught it for a number of years and came to believe in the wisdom of looking back to where we have been to get to our present state. Only then can we chart a course into the future.

Sometimes I feel like that old Charlie Brown joke. Lucy said to Charlie Brown, "Charlie Brown, are you a futurist, someone who sailing on the ship of life likes to set you deck chair on the front of the ship to see into the future, to see where we are going. Or, are you a person who likes to sit your deck chair on the back end of the ship to see where we have been, to trace our steps that brought us to this place in history. Where do you want to sit your deck chair, Charlie Brown." Charlie Brown responds, "Actually, I haven't been able to get my deck chair unfolded yet."

Ahhh, history. I do love it.

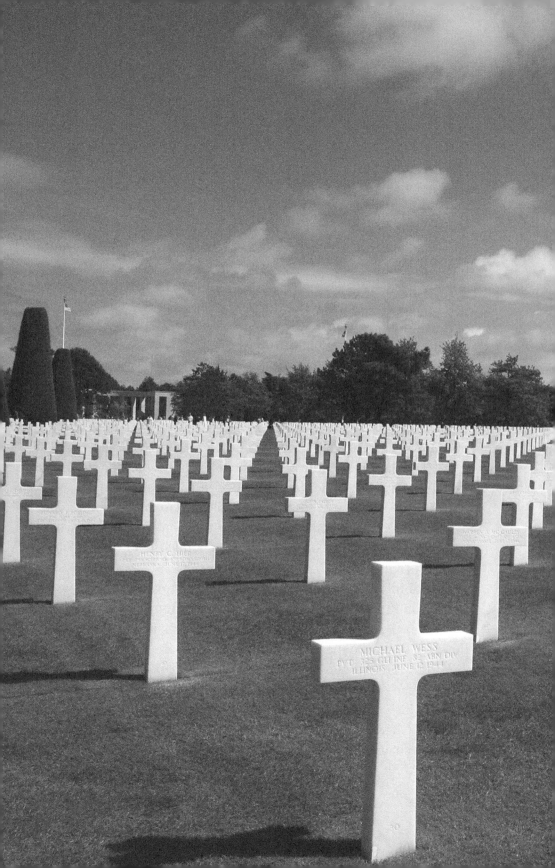

DUNKIRK

A movie about one of the most amazing deliverance miracles in history is sweeping the country. Dunkirk is one of the greatest events of World War II and the movie tells the story of 500,000 British, French, and Belgium soldiers surrounded by the German army in a hopeless situation. Braving great danger, the British people rallied to their rescue, saved the day and, perhaps, the war.

Watching this movie puts you at ground zero for the terror which never let up for a full ninety minutes. The Nazi army had charged through Belgium and into France against troops that were ill-equipped and ill-trained to meet the German assault. The Magi-

The British people rallied to their rescue, saved the day and, perhaps, the war.

not Line, built by France to provide a first line of defense in case the Germans attacked again as they did in WWI, had been constructed with its heavy guns all facing to the east. The German army came around the Maginot Line and entered France very quickly making the French defenses useless.

In a short ten days, From May 10th to May 20th of 1940, German troops had the allies surrounded and began pushing them back toward the English Channel. The three armies, British, French, and Belgium, found themselves on the beach north of Dunkirk with virtually no food or water and without the means to protect themselves from the German Air Force.

It was at the point of "no hope," that the tide began to turn for the allied soldiers. A flood of more than 800 small boats left Dover, England for the beaches of Dunkirk. They braved a mined channel, German submarines, and constant harassment by enemy planes to travel the 60 miles across the always treacherous English Channel to carry their troops home. One British naval officer looking out at the dots on the horizon coming in from the north was asked, "What do you see?" He responded with a smile, "Hope, I see hope."

The parade of small boats from England continued for eight days carrying more than 325,000 soldiers from Dunkirk and another 150,000 from Calais, Amiens, and Lille. One soldier said, "When we saw the white cliffs of Dover in the distance it was like going from Hell to Heaven. You knew a miracle had happened." The Allies lost almost 80,000 dead and captured. Also lost was virtually all of the means to fight including guns, tanks, ammunition, and fuel. From a humanitarian perspective the evacuation from Dunkirk was a miracle. From a military perspective it was a disaster. So much of the necessary material of war was lost that Great Britain's ability to carry on was in question.

The disaster at Dunkirk motivated the United States to offer war materials through its lend-lease plan that would support any government fighting the Nazis. There was great resistance in our Congress to getting involved in any way with the war going on in Europe but Roosevelt kept the pressure on and it passed Congress by a narrow vote.

At the end of the movie when the evacuation was over and British troops were on a train into the interior of England, one of the soldiers found a newspaper. From it he read the report of Prime Minister Churchill's famous, "We shall never give up," speech.

"We shall fight in France, we shall fight on the seas and oceans, we shall fight with growing confidence and growing strength in the air, we shall defend our island, whatever the cost may be. We shall fight on the beaches, we shall fight on the landing grounds, we shall fight in the fields and in the streets, we shall fight in the hills: we shall never surrender."

The only thing missing from that reading was that it did not come with the raspy voice of Prime Minister Churchill himself. Surely no one ever delivered a stronger statement nor a better speech.

If you see Dunkirk, it will affect you. You will not soon forget.

AMERICA'S DUNKIRK

A few weeks back I wrote a column about Dunkirk, the miraculous British escape early in the Second World War. A friend who spent his working career teaching history in Long Island, New York pointed out to me that we had our own "Dunkirk" during the Revolutionary War. It was called the Battle of Long Island.

The date was August 27, 1776. George Washington and his patriots had just come from a successful effort against the British in Massachusetts where his new army had fought the British to a draw.

He moved the bulk of his troops, more than 19,000 of them, to Manhattan Island where he hoped to defend New York City from the British. The British plan was to take New York and split New England from the more southern colonies. They could then use the Hudson River to bring reinforcements and war materials down from Canada.

Washington's army made their escape into New Jersey and withdrew into Pennsylvania.

The battle preparations developed for more than six weeks. The U.S. troops occupied Brooklyn Heights while the British brought in more and more reinforcements. Finally, the British had more than 32,000 troops, including 9000 German mercenaries, and an astounding 150 ships surrounding Manhattan Island. Washington's main army was much smaller but had created intricate defensive positions that made them difficult to breach.

The British attacked the U.S. positions from two directions and after forty-eight hours of fierce fighting forced Washington and his outnumbered troops from their positions. The U.S. Army found themselves fighting a rear guard action that slowed the British advance but soon they were backed up to the East River.

It was at the point that the heroes of the Battle of Long Island began to appear. One group, called the Maryland 400, though there were only around 270 men in their company, became the major rear guard to protect the retreat. They were led by Major Mordecai Gist. They inflicted great causalities on the British and sacrificed themselves almost to a man to protect the bulk of the U.S. troops. In then end only 12 made it back to their battle lines.

General Washington found himself backed up to the East River with General William Howe's British regulars surrounding his beleaguered army. Night fell and the British settled to rest through the night for the final push the next day. In the meantime General Washington had put out a call for every flat bottomed boat available from across the East River in New Jersey to come to their aid. Hundreds rallied to their plight. To mask the withdrawal Washington ordered that the fires in his camp be kept burning all night so the British would think they were still there.

Washington had about two thirds of his army across the East River when dawn broke the next morning. Had the British ships surrounding the island been able to see what was happening they would have sailed in and cut off their escape. But, as often happens at important times, fate stepped in and a heavy fog enveloped the East River. The British could not see the many small boats on the river. Washington made his escape into New Jersey and continued his withdrawal into Pennsylvania. His army was preserved to fight another day. Four months later, on Christmas Eve, Washington brought his army across the Delaware River and defeated the German mercenaries at Trenton, New Jersey, the first major victory for the embattled U.S. Army.

The evacuation of 19,000 U.S. troops from Long Island does not compare with the several hundred thousand British troops evacuated from Dunkirk 165 years later. However, considering that Washington's troops were the bulk of the U.S. Army at the time, it was a major accomplishment that was of immense importance in the eventual success of the Revolutionary War.

As Walter Cronkite used to say, "What kind of day was it? It was a day like all days, and you were there."

HISTORY SPEAKS TO US ON OUR PRESENT ECONOMIC SITUATION

By all modern measures the recession is over. Unfortunately, some segments of our economy are still feeling the effects. Unemployment is still an issue, especially among lower skilled jobs. And, growth in the manufacturing sector lags well behind the ideal. Most of the political-speak from Washington DC these days ignores both the reality of our situation and our history. I believe in history. History is the only reality available to us for future planning. We must study history, as they say, or we are doomed to repeat it.

Some say that we can solve our problems by cutting taxes and slashing government spending. However, taxes in the United States as a percentage of Gross Domestic Product (GDP) are at their lowest level since 1950. The countries of to-day's world with lower unemployment and higher rates of economic growth all have much higher taxes than the USA. Germany and Denmark are good examples.

Governments are the only entities with the capability to "position" countries in the international marketplace.

Others espouse that the government should withdraw from various aspects of the economy to create a "free market." Yet, the fastest growing economy in the world is China that has almost total governmental control of its economy. Governments are the only entities with the capability to "position" countries in the international marketplace. Both The Sudan and Brazil are good examples of countries with little government involvement and they have run away economies and very high inflation.

Most would identify the "cut taxes" and "free market" solutions to our current problem as based on "conservative" thinking. Conservative theorists Edmund Burke and writers William Buckley and George Will would disagree, based on knowledge of the history of our economy and that of the rest of the world

Both the Bureau of Labor Statistics and the Tax Policy Center show for the past 60 years whenever tax rates were the highest, more jobs were created than when the tax rates were the lowest, as they are now.

In a time of previous economic difficulty, with multiple Republicans, (Eisenhower, Nixon, Ford, and Reagan) in the White House, the response from Washington DC was very different. From 1957, the year of Sputnik, to the early 1980s when U.S. taxes were significantly higher than now the government created the Interstate Highway System, made massive investments in education and science, created small business incubators and built bridges to the rest of the world for trade. The result was major development in science and business, major improvements in the education and health industries, fifty years of economic growth, and the highest living standard in the world.

Getting control of government spending may be helpful in solving our current crisis but cutting taxes is not the route to a healthy economy. Every time we have cut taxes in recent history we have moved further from a healthy economy and deeper into debt. History speaks to us. We should listen.

LOOKING AT THE NATIONAL DEBT
FROM AN HISTORICAL PERSPECTIVE

Well, here we are again. The government is trying to recover from a partial shut-down and the debt limit problem has been put off for another three months. Held hostage in this sordid affair were many federal employees, multiple government functions, and having enough money to pay our debts. Republicans justify their actions saying they must protect the public from the tax and spend Democrats while the Democrats say they have an election mandate for their actions. Who is right?

One of my favorite politicians was Everett Dirksen, the long-time Senator from Illinois. He was known for his long speeches full of sound bites for radio and television. In a budget debate in Congress, Senator Dirksen said, "Well, a million here and a million there and the first thing you know it runs into real money."

That is where we are today and it isn't millions, it's trillions.

That is where we are today as a country, into real money and it isn't billions, it's trillions. The Republicans blame the Democrats and the Democrats blame the Republicans. Who is at fault? Let's look at the history of our national debt. For clarity, let's not deal with the Obama administration since it is not yet over. New depths may be plumbed and new records set between now and 2016.

Since 1950 only three presidential terms experienced reduced national debt. The terms were administered by Presidents Harry Truman in the 1940's, Jimmy Carter in the late 1970s, and Bill Clinton in the 1990s. All three were Democrats.

Of the other 9 presidents since 1950, three reduced the amount of deficit when compared to their predecessors. Those three also were Democrats. The six remaining presidents had increased deficits that added significantly to the national debt. All six of those presidents were Republicans. The worst records belong to Ronald Reagan (+20.6 percent), G.H.W. Bush (+15.0 percent) and GW Bush

(+27.1 percent). Of course, both Bushes were fighting wars and Reagan was fighting the cold war, so one shouldn't oversimplify cause and effect.

Who added the most federal employees? Ronald Reagan. Who spent the most per capita on welfare programs? Again, it was Ronald Reagan. Who had the greatest percentage of deficit spending? George W. Bush wins that honor.

Between the Carter Administration in 1980 and the beginning of the Obama administration in 2009, the national debt rose 40.6 percent and 36.4 percent of that growth occurred while Republicans were in the White House. So much for the fiscal conservative label worn by our recent Republican presidents. And, the Republican label for the opposition party as "tax-and-spend" Democrats may be misapplied.

When you began reading, is this the way your thought it would come out? Me neither.

PATRIOTIC SPEECHES THAT RESONATE

I love a great speech. We have all heard a thousand speeches in our lifetime. Independence Day celebrations like those that are going on all across the nation this week have their speech makers. Some speeches are inspirational and others are just, "deadly." Many slide into the deep recesses of our mind, never to be heard from again. However, there are some that grab you and never let go.

Every history student knows of Patrick Henry's speech that ended with the memorable words, "as for me, give me liberty or give me death." He delivered that speech just before the revolution with Great Britain that created a nation out of thirteen colonies.

Abraham Lincoln delivered several speeches that grabbed the psyche of America

Some just grab you and never let go.

in the tumultuous Civil War years. Many are still quoted such as his Gettysburg Address that began, "Four score and seven years ago," and ends with, "…that government of the people, by the people, for the people, shall not perish from the earth." Other quotations from Lincoln, both profound and humorous, include….

"A house divided against itself cannot stand."

"Most folks are as happy as they make up their minds to be."

"If I was two-faced, would I be wearing this one?"

"The people will save their government, if the government will allow them."

"What kills a skunk is the publicity it gives itself."

Great speech makers during my lifetime include Dr. Martin Luther King, Jr. and President John F. Kennedy. King delivered the famous "I have a Dream" speech that is a part of the American lexicon. Who could forget the phrases that impressed that speech on the American conscience?

"We refuse to believe that the bank of justice is bankrupt. We refuse to believe that there are insufficient funds in the great vault of opportunity.

"I have a dream today that my four little children will one day live in a nation where they will not be judged by the color of their skin but by the content of their character.

"When we allow freedom to ring, when we let it ring from every village and hamlet, from every state and every city we will be able to speed up the day when all of God's children will be able to join hands and sing......

"Free at last, free at last, thank God Almighty, we are free at last."

One could argue whether King or John F. Kennedy was better at making a memorable speech. With their different styles they were hard to compare. Content and delivery are equally important in giving memorable speeches and King and Kennedy were great at both.

President Kennedy's first inaugural address burst into our consciousness with sentences that resonated like.....

"We observe today not a victory of party but a celebration of freedom."

"...symbolizing an end as well as a beginning, signifying renewal as well as change."

"Let every nation know, whether it wishes us well or ill, that we shall pay any price, bear any burden, meet any hardship, support any friend, oppose any foe, to assure the survival and the success of liberty."

"Let us never negotiate out of fear, but let us never fear to negotiate."

"...and so, my fellow Americans, ask not what your country can do for you; ask what you can do for your country.

Every great speech has a beginning that captures the audience and an ending that delivers a message designed to stay with you. That "ask not" line was Kennedy's challenge to America, one we still have before us, one that still challenges us.

If you are praying for our nation and I hope you are, pray for inspired leaders with the soul of our nation in their heart. Pray they have the best of American ideals in their minds, and can challenge us with a vision for tomorrow.

THE GREAT COMPROMISER

Repeal Obamacare. Repeal Roe vs. Wade. Get rid of restrictions on the development of energy resources. Cancel ecology regulations. Build a wall on our southern border. Fully fund Medicare. Pass a balanced budget. Fund medical and scientific research. Save Social Security. It is a formidable list, though not exhaustive. The question is, will any of these major goals of one or another of our political parties actually move through our legislative process and become law?

One man made his mark on our nation in the 19th century by negotiating compromise.

The realists among us know that none of these desires of our political parties will become law without the willingness to compromise extreme positions and move to middle ground. The question for us and for our leadership in Washington DC is, "Who will step up and lead the way to compromise, to actions beneficial to the people, to getting rid of gridlock in Congress?"

History is full of statesmen who made great contributions. George Washington we revere as the Father of our Country, Abraham Lincoln as The Great Emancipator for freeing the slaves, and Franklin D. Roosevelt took the country at its lowest point and breathed life back into our economy. Did we ever have a person whose greatest contribution was providing leadership in the solution of problems through compromise? Indeed we did.

One man made his mark on our nation in the 19th century by negotiating compromise. He was known as "The Great Compromiser." His name was Daniel Webster. No, he isn't the guy who created our dictionary. That was Noah Webster. Daniel Webster lived during one of the most tumultuous times in our history. He was born in 1782 and served our country both in the Senate and as Secretary of State from 1830 to 1852. During that twenty-two year period there were many major conflicts, several of which required compromises in order to avert war.

Daniel Webster was our negotiator with Canada and Great Britain over the border between Canada and the state of Maine. The Webster-Ashburton Treaty averted a third war with Great Britain and Canada over that contested border. The treaty was created by compromise. Both sides gave up something they wanted in order to reach agreement. That treaty also created the U.S. and Canadian border through the middle of the Great Lakes and guaranteed free navigation for both countries on those inland waterways.

President Andrew Jackson and Congress had a significant conflict over the function and responsibility of a National Bank in 1832. Daniel Webster affected a compromise that, while not providing either side with what they wanted, gave enough to create The National Bank. Though The National Bank died in 1836 it became the model and forerunner of our Federal Reserve System that re-emerged in the 20th century and still functions today as a stabilizing influence on our financial institutions.

Perhaps the most famous of Webster's accomplishments was called The Compromise of 1850. It settled a disagreement between the Southern and Northern States regarding the status of the territories won in the war with Mexico, (1846-1848). Henry Clay (Kentucky) and John C. Calhoun (South Carolina) almost came to blows over the disposition of the new territories until Daniel Webster stepped in with a compromise that allowed some territories to have slaves, others not, and a third region to have control over whether or not slaves were to be permitted. Had this compromise not been effected it is likely that the Civil War, fought in the 1860s, would have been fought many years earlier.

The point of the foregoing is that we could use Daniel Webster or someone with his capabilities in this tumultuous time. We have watched the U.S. Congress live with gridlock for much of the past six years. The political far right and far left remain at ideological swords points. Neither can see merit in the positions or proposals of the other. The art of politics is the art of compromise. We need another great compromiser like Daniel Webster.

VJ DAY: THE END OF WWII

It is hard to remember what was happening seven decades ago but those who experienced it will never forget. World War II began for us when Japan attacked Pearl Harbor and almost destroyed our entire Pacific fleet. The loss of men and women, ships and planes, and peace of mind is hard to describe today. Take the aftermath of 9-11 and multiply it exponentially. This week, on August 14th, we celebrate Victory in Japan, VJ Day.

In 1941 Europe had already been at war for eighteen months and the U.S. had carefully stayed out of it. After Pearl Harbor we could no longer ignore the necessity to fight along-side of our allies and so we tooled up all of our industrial might and jumped in with both feet. The military strategy was to pool our resources with the European nations and defeat the Nazi war machine first, then to go to Asia to face off with Japan.

There were, literally, thousands of people there working on the Atomic Bomb.

The Pacific War was fought first as a delaying action and then as an island by island advance toward the Japanese mainland. Casualties were high and real estate laboriously won until the end came suddenly in August of 1945.

My father was a handicapped mid-lifer during those war years. He was not acceptable for the military because of having lost an arm in a hunting accident at the age of 15. Still, he was up to his neck in the war effort. He managed food service facilities for the war department. His last war-time assignment was in Oak Ridge, Tennessee where the Manhattan project had been on-going since 1942. There were, literally, thousands of people there working on the nation's most top secret project, the development of the Atomic Bomb.

Our little family of four was living on a hill side in Oak Ridge when the bomb was dropped on Hiroshima. Until that day the workers in Oak Ridge did not know what their project was. When it

exploded on the other side of the Pacific it reverberated through the hills of rural Tennessee and, suddenly, everyone knew. People came out of those ultra-secret work camps surrounding Oak Ridge with a collective shout that must have been heard all the way to Washington DC.

I shall never forget the noise, confusion, and utter jubilation of that celebration when the people raised their voices together to celebrate that the war was over and they had a hand in the final outcome. It was an amazing experience. It is good for us to remember times like those when everyone stood shoulder to shoulder working toward a common goal, when anything other than total victory was unthinkable. It is good to remember VJ Day.

WHERE IS OLD HARRY
WHEN WE NEED HIM?

I was raised in Missouri and was taught that Harry S. Truman, the 33rd president of the United States, was a Patron Saint. Well, perhaps he wasn't a saint in the most Catholic sense but he was a saint to most Missourians. Old, "Give 'em hell, Harry" as he was called in some quarters, was known for many "common man" traits.

He liked to pour his hot coffee from his cup into his saucer and blow on it, then pour it back into the cup. That is not a practice for "polite" company but it is certainly a practical approach to cooling down your coffee. And, old Harry was known to be a practical man. He had a sign on his desk that said, "The buck stops here."

He had a sign on his desk that said, "The buck stops here."

It was his reminder that eventually someone had to make a decision and he was the final decider. He was not one for letting a decision linger.

Harry Truman's presidency was one of conflict from the time he assumed the presidency in the final six months of WWII until he left office in January of 1953 in the midst of the Korean War. In between, he fired General Douglas MacArthur, one of our most popular war heroes, and faced off with two of the strongest unions in the country forcing them to continue working even though they had voted to strike. When President Truman and his wife Bess had served their last day in the White House and left for home in Missouri, there was no crowd seeing him off at the train station in Washington DC. His popularity rating was an all- time low at 22%. He was sure he would be remembered as a failed president.

Instead, history has treated him very well. His accomplishments were many and some were precedent setting. He continued the lend-lease plan that supported England during the final years of WWII, made the all -important decision to use the atomic bomb to end the war with Japan, helped create the United Nations, and authored the plan to rebuild Europe after the Great War was over. For those reasons and other he is revered today as one of our top ten presidents.

Who could forget the famous Chicago Tribune headline in 1948 that said, "Dewey Defeats Truman?" In truth, I'm not sure anyone ever defeated Harry Truman. He was his own man from beginning to end and he made an art form out of doing what he thought was right for the American people.

President Truman was not known as a great speech maker but there is one I would like to call attention to today. It was given on December 15, 1952 at the National Archives to dedicate a shrine that held the original Constitution and several other major documents. He said, "The Constitution expresses an idea that belongs to the people, the idea of the free man. What this idea means may vary from time to time. There was a time when people believed that the Constitution meant that men could not be prevented from exploiting child labor or paying sweatshop wages. We no longer believe those things. We have discovered that the Constitution does not prevent us from correcting social injustice, or advancing the general welfare. The idea of freedom which is embodied in these great documents has overcome all attempts to turn them into a rigid set of rules to suppress freedom."

In short, he told us that the Constitution lives and breathes; it is a Constitution of principles and not of rules and regulations. From time to time we need someone like old Harry to remind us of the genius of our founding fathers and the brilliance of the words by which we are governed. If only Harry were still around to give 'em hell from time to time when they need it.

8

IMMIGRATION

President Franklin Roosevelt called The United States a "melting pot," and he was right. Virtually everyone who came to these shores from the beginning until the 21st century came from someplace else. The Statue of Liberty standing at the edge of the harbor in New York City has a plaque that provides an invitation to immigrants from around the globe:

"Give me your tired, your poor, your huddled masses yearning to breathe free, the wretched refuse of your teeming shore. Send them, the homeless, tempest-tossed to me. I lift my lamp beside the golden door."

For more than 100 years we opened the doors of America to anyone who wanted to come. Then, we began closing the door little by little. Today, we allow approximately one million people who come into the country to stay each year. Another 70 million come to visit. They come, literally, from all over the world, from every continent and almost every country.

Immigration is important to the United States for a number of reasons. First, it makes up for the fact that the birth rate in American families has dropped from 2.5 children to 1.2 over the past fifty years. Most of Europe is experiencing the same problem and they are experiencing a drop in population. The United States has stayed even in the recent past primarily because of the influx of immigrants.

Our economy depends on two key factors to remain productive and growing. They are continued technological development and population stability. With more than 3000 colleges and universities working on research across the country, continued technological development is almost a "given." Population, however, is the big questions mark. We need immigration at the one million mark or above to keep our population stable.

Much of the focus of a new political administration has been on illegal immigration. In recent weeks the rhetoric has swung over into the entire immigration program with changes proposed that may significantly alter the number of immigrants into the country. I am reminded of that old southern saying, "When all is said and done, more will be said than done." In politics, this statement will hold true most of the time. However, any discussion of immigration is, indeed, a serious discussion.

FINALLY GETTING
ILLEGAL IMMIGRATION RIGHT

After two years in office President Obama recently gave himself a report card on the fulfilling of his campaign promises. Chief among the negatives was finding a resolution of the illegal immigration problem, the eleven million illegals who are currently in the U.S. and the throngs who continue to cross our borders without proper papers.

The problem is complicated and almost impossible to solve which is why our representatives in Washington, D.C. have had so much difficulty reaching a compromise solution to the on-going problem. Much of the public discussion is focused on our southern border and the constant flow of Mexican nationals across our border into Texas, New Mexico, Arizona, and California. This is a stretch of geography that extends more than 1500 miles across desert and mountains that is almost impossible to patrol much less control.

In the absence of positive and definitive leadership on the part of the federal government on this important issue, we should applaud the efforts of the states who have taken action.

Millions of dollars have already been spent on building a fence, doubling and tripling the number of border patrols, and traveling to both sides of the border to meet and discuss the problem with various officials representing both Mexico and the U.S. The results have not been impressive. Knowledgeable people tell us that a complete closing of that vulnerable border will have little effect. The Rio Grand River and the rest of our southern border can be compared to the military defense line created by France after WWI to protect them from the Germans. When Hitler decided to invade France at the beginning of WWII, his tanks simply choose a different route, rolled down the super highway that ran from Berlin to Paris and were in Paris in 30 days. Does anyone think that closing our southern border will have a better result? Even if one could close the southern border we have three other borders to the east, west, and north that are far more extensive and difficult to control than the one between the U.S. and Mexico.

Further, the illegal immigration issues are far more complex than just closing the borders. We have B-1 visas given to tourist to visit the U.S., F-1 visas for University students, J-1 Visas for temporary teachers, researchers, workers, and others that have varying expiration dates. The rules of all of these are regularly violated with impunity. Proper enforcement of our laws is years and billions of dollars away.

Considering the issues, the complications, and the costs how can we solve this seemingly impossible problem? Closing our southern border is not the answer. There is no one answer, no one action that can be taken to solve the problem. In short, if the illegal immigrants want to come, we can't stop them. To solve the problem we have to make them not want to come. The solution is in the answer to one question, "What motivates the steady stream of illegal immigrants to violate our laws and take great personal risks to come to The U.S.?" The answer to that question is obvious, the usually "hot" economy that provides work, money, and the best standard of living in the world. What attracts ants to a picnic? Immigrants, legal or illegal, are attracted to the wealth, opportunity, and hope that is the American Dream.

Where should we start to control the flow of illegal immigrants? Start with the businesses and industries that are the source of the jobs and opportunity. Do we need new laws to enforce. Maybe, but maybe not. Do we need to enforce the laws we have. Absolutely.

What should we do first? We should transfer the useless expenditures for the Mexican border fence to enforcing our employment laws. We should increase our vigilance regarding who is employed, who is working, and who the employers are who are complicit in the violation of our laws.

Will that solve the problem? No, not totally, but it will begin to exclude the ants from the picnic and it will begin to control the key factor that provides the motivation for illegals coming to the U.S.

What should we do about the eleven million illegal immigrants who are already here? The reason the illegals are here is the same reason more continue to come; jobs, opportunities, and hope. If we shut down the availability of illegal jobs we will see many illegals begin to exit the country for better opportunities elsewhere.

Will we find many of these newly out of work people in our federal training and welfare programs? The answer is an obvious "Yes" but those are both places where illegals can be identified, regulated and in many cases sent home.

Should all illegals be deported? No. Many of them should stay. But those who receive this amnesty should be in necessary jobs and should show evidence of assimilation in terms of language development and other bench marks that they have made progress in becoming a productive part of American society.

The title of this essay is "Getting Illegal Immigration Right". The reason for the title relates to the positive "happenings" in forty-one of our states who, in the absence of federal action on this crucial issue, have enacted their own legislation in the past year. The overall focus of many of these legislative efforts is the job market and our employment laws. In the absence of positive and definitive federal leadership on this important issue, we should applaud the efforts of the states who have taken action. They are finally trying to get it right.

IMMIGRATION:
CORRECTING MISTAKES OF THE PAST

I am writing this in the midst of the furor of the Immigration Ban instituted by President Trump in early February of 2017. Before this column was printed the courts spoke on that issue and put a "hold" on President Trump's ban. It is likely this case will make its way to the Supreme Court. Whatever the resolution of this situation, it is obvious that our immigration policies are being closely scrutinized and may face significant changes.

A bit of history is in order. In the first half of the 20th century the way our immigration policy was written was patently discriminatory. At the time we followed the Immigration Act of 1924 which restricted immigration on the basis of national origin. Specifically, those from Africa and Asia had difficulty entering the country while those from Europe were given preference. John F. Kennedy was a major critic of this policy calling it "racist and prejudiced, not at all in keeping with our principles and values." Senator Ted Kennedy said, "If we change this policy to consider all locations of national origin as equal it would have little effect on the racial and ethnic make-up of our country." The new policy was signed into law in 1968 by President Lyndon Johnson. It created major changes in how immigrants were allowed into the country.

> "We need to think about what kind of a country we want."
>
> Anne Geyer

President Kennedy was right as per the prejudice that was innate in the 1924 Law. Senator Ted Kennedy was wrong because the change in the law that occurred in 1968 significantly altered a number of key aspects of our society including where immigrants came from, why they were allowed into the country, and where they settled after they arrived here. Our inner cities, always enclaves of ethnic groups, became more so. National groups such as the Mexican and Central American immigrants became voting blocks in key areas of our country. In short, the Immigration and Nationality Act of 1965 changed America. The new law was much less prejudice and that was good but, as my grandmother used to say, it "threw out the baby with the bath water."

Two major changes in the law resulted in much of the problem. First, with the new law in 1968, being a family member of a citizen or Green Card holder in the U.S. became a major criteria for entry. Second, the provision in the 1924 law that gave preference to professionals and individuals with special skills was dropped. In short, our emphasis became "family," as opposed to adding to the U.S. economic engine which had been a key criteria prior to the passage of the new law.

Because immigration increased dramatically from Africa, Asia, South and Central America, parts of the world with limited educational opportunities, we increased the lower economic classes in the country exponentially while not improving U.S. economic capability. This put a strain on schools, the welfare system, health services, etc. It did not improve our ability to compete in the world marketplace.

So, how do we recreate the economic stimulus of immigration while not sliding back into the provisions of discrimination that dominated our immigration policies in the first half of the 20th century? It is a tough question.

Anne Geyer, a newspaper columnist and observer of the American dynamic for more than fifty years, counseled our Washington DC leadership in a recent column. She said, "We need to think about what kind of country we want; what foreign cultures can best enrich ours; and how our laws and institutions can best accommodate newcomers, without American losing its own, unique soul."

There is a saying that rings true at this juncture of history here in America. The original quotation came from no less an international genius than Mohandas K. Gandhi. He said, "We have to not only do the right thing, we have to do it the right way." Amen and Amen.

THE SOUTHERN WALL?
ANOTHER BOONDOGGLE

Twice in the past week President Trump has promised that we are going to build the wall along our southern border. Twice, he has played to the balcony for approval but has avoided the reality that the proposed wall is a boondoggle. The wall will cost billions but won't solve our illegal immigration problem.

Much of the public discussion on illegal immigration is focused on our southern border and the constant flow of Central American nationals across our border into Texas, New Mexico, Arizona, and California. This is a stretch of geography that extends more than 1500 miles across desert and mountains that is almost impossible to patrol much less control. Millions of dollars have already been spent building a fence and quadrupling the number of border patrols. Knowledgeable people tell us that a complete closing of that vulnerable border will have little effect.

> No ten foot fence will ever defeat an eleven foot ladder

The Rio Grande and the rest of our Southern border can be likened to the military defense line created by France after WWI to protect them from Germany. When Hitler invaded France at the beginning of WWII, his tanks simply choose a different route, rolled down the super highway and were in Paris in 30 days. No wall in history has ever had much success keeping people out and that includes Hadrian's Wall in England, the Berlin Wall in Germany, and the Great Wall of China. Some smart person said, "No ten foot fence will ever defeat an eleven foot ladder."

We can close our Southern border but we have other borders to the East, West, and North. They are far more extensive and difficult to control than the one between the U.S. and Mexico. Anyone who has ever fished the coasts of the southeast or southwest U.S. knows the impossibility of patrolling and/or controlling the many inlets and swamp areas along our eastern and western borders. Our northern border with Canada is worse yet. It is the longest unenforced border in the world. One can easily fly into Vancouver, BC, Canada and hire a taxi for a $20 taxi ride out along the border highway. At some point one can leave the taxi and walk south for twenty minutes and be in the United States. So much for border security.

In short, if the illegal immigrants want to come, we can't stop them. To solve the problem we have to make them not want to come. That key is in the answer to one question, "What motivates illegal immigrants to violate our laws to come to The U.S.?" The answer is obvious. It is the U.S. economy that provides work, money, and the best standard of living in the world. Immigrants, legal or illegal, are attracted to the wealth, opportunity, and hope that is the American Dream.

Where should we start to control the flow of illegal immigrants? Start with the businesses and industries that are the source of the jobs and opportunity. We should increase our vigilance regarding who is employed and who the employers are who are complicit in the violation of our laws. Violators should be prosecuted to the fullest extent of the law.

Just a portion of the money we are planning to spend on the wall should be used to beef up the Immigration and Naturalization Service. They are responsible to track the more than 70 million visitors who come to the U.S. from other countries each year. A full forty percent of those currently in the U.S. illegally came into the country with a visitor's visa and just stayed. At present, the INS does not have the mechanism or the manpower to keep track of those who come to visit.

The sooner we get focused on what is attracting illegal immigrants, the sooner we can get a handle on this problem. Folks, the key issue isn't our borders, it is enforcing our laws in the work place.

THE SOUTHERN BORDER WALL: WHY NOT?

A few weeks back I wrote a column entitled, "The Southern Border Wall: Another Boondoggle?" Many wrote to support my contention that such a border wall is a waste of money, time and effort. However, a few wanted a more through explanation. Here it is.

History teachers us the border wall won't work. Walls never work. That includes Hadrian's Wall in England, The Great Wall of China, and the Berlin Wall. People who want to get over or around a wall just find another way.

"It won't accomplish its purpose and will prove to be impossible to build."

Texas Governor Rick Perry

George W. Bush proposed building a wall back in 2005 which he anticipated would cost five billion dollars. Today, that proposed cost has ballooned by some estimates to more than thirty billion. But, money isn't our problem. Our government owns a printing press. (Isn't Mexico going to pay for it anyway?) The problem is that a wall just isn't practical. The experts who have tried to find a way to make such a wall work have mostly given up. Janet Napolitano, former Secretary of Homeland Security, worked on the fence from 2009 until 2013. She said, "It has never worked as planned. I will freeze all funding for the border fence." Governor Rick Perry of Texas who has 900 miles of the border in his state opposed the wall from the beginning saying, "It won't accomplish its purpose and will prove to be impossible to build."

Even if it would eventually work, most of us won't live to see it. Why not? Building the wall is not just a construction job. If it was we could haul some equipment down there and put up a wall in a few months. So, what is the problem? The problem is that we live in a democracy where people have property rights. The government can't just step in and take whatever they want without due process.

The Bush border wall proposal was sent to Congress in

September of 2006. It passed by an overwhelming majority in both houses of Congress. Once the plan was in place and the parcels of land identified that would need to be purchased, the legal issues began to materialize. More than 345 legal processes were involved. Most were related to "eminent domain," the law that allows government to take land for the public good, for fair compensation. Of course, what is fair compensation to the government may not at all appear fair to the person who owns the land. The first law suit was filed eleven years ago. Today, more than a decade later, we still have 80 law suits pending related to the first series of land parcels. Conservative estimates are that the land parcels for the rest of the wall may generate as many as 750 more legal issues.

If it has taken us eleven years to get to the last 80 law suits and we anticipate 750 more. Can we project anything less than another fifteen to twenty years before construction can start on the wall? (At least it gives Mexico time to save their money.)

Folks, both history and logic tell us that our problem with illegal immigration cannot be solved with a wall. We have four borders to protect, not just one. The other three are greater problems to enforce than the one between the U.S. and Mexico. Consider, also, if we did have secure borders we still have the problem that a full 40 percent of those in the country illegally, came here with legal visas and just stayed.

The only way to solve our dilemma is by enforcing our work place laws. Illegal immigrants have to eat like the rest of us. If they can't find work they will not come. If they do come and can't find work, they will not stay.

To summarize, the southern wall project is a boondoggle because of property acquisition problems, construction, and cost issues. But, most of all because Texas Governor Rick Perry was right, it won't work.

THE ILLEGAL IMMIGRATION ARGUMENT

The presidential campaign of 2016 is already in full swing and the primary issues have crystallized. Chief among these is what to do about illegal immigration and about the estimated eleven million illegals hiding just below the surface in our country.

The problems related to illegal immigration are complicated to solve which is why our representatives in Washington DC have had so much difficulty reaching a solution to this on-going problem. Much of the public discussion is focused on our southern border and the constant flow of Mexican nationals across our border into Texas, New Mexico, Arizona, and California. This is a stretch of geography that extends more than 1500 miles across desert and mountains that is almost impossible to patrol much less control.

Millions of dollars have already been spent building a fence and quadrupling the number of border patrols.

Millions of dollars have already been spent building a fence and quadrupling the number of border patrols. Our leaders have traveled to both sides of the border to meet and discuss the problem with various officials representing both Mexico and the U.S. Knowledgeable people tell us that a complete closing of that vulnerable border will have little effect. The Rio Grande and the rest of our Southern border can be likened to the military defense line created by France after WWI to protect them from the Germans. When Hitler decided to invade France at the beginning of WWII, his tanks simply choose a different route, rolled own the super highway and they were in Paris in 30 days. No wall in history has ever had much success keeping people out and that includes Hadrian's Wall in England, the Berlin Wall in Germany, and the Great Wall of China. Some smart person said, "No ten foot fence will ever defeat an eleven foot ladder."

We can close our Southern border but we have other borders

to the East, West, and North. They are far more extensive and difficult to control than the one between the U.S. and Mexico.

In short, if the illegal immigrants want to come, we can't stop them. To solve the problem we have to make them not want to come. That key is in the answer to one question, "What motivates illegal immigrants to violate our laws and take great personal risks to come to The U.S.?" The answer is obvious. It is the U.S. economy that provides work, money, and the best standard of living in the world. Immigrants, legal or illegal, are attracted to the wealth, opportunity, and hope that is the American Dream. It's the same thing that attracts ants to a picnic?

Where should we start to control the flow of illegal immigrants? Start with the businesses and industries that are the source of the jobs and opportunity. Do we need new laws to enforce? We may, but maybe not. Do we need to enforce the laws we have? Absolutely. We should increase our vigilance regarding who is employed and who the employers are who are complicit in the violation of our laws. And, we should prosecute the violators to the fullest extent of the law. Will that solve the problem? No, not totally, but it will begin to discourage the ants from the picnic.

What should we do about the eleven million illegal immigrants who are already here? Again, the issue is jobs. If we shut down the availability of jobs for undocumented workers we will see many of them exit the country for better opportunities elsewhere.

Should all illegals be deported? No. Many of them should stay but those who receive this "amnesty" should be in necessary jobs and should show evidence of assimilation. This should include language development and other bench marks that show they have made progress in becoming a productive part of American society.

The sooner we get focused on what is attracting illegal immigrants, the sooner we can get a handle on this problem. Folks, the key issue isn't our borders, it is enforcing our laws in the work place.

9

HEALTH CARE

Perhaps no issue touches all of America like health care. From the cradle to the grave we are constantly in need of the services provided by our health care industry. Doctors and nurses are the most visible practitioners within health care but the list of others who provide services to us seems interminable. From researchers to insurance people, from X-ray technicians to laboratory workers, from hospital personnel to medical specialist, the list goes on and on.

President Trump said, "Whoever thought health care could be so complicated." Well, duh! The more moving parts in a machine the more complicated the repair. Health Care is a very large umbrella with hundreds/thousands of moving parts.

Four presidents from Truman to Reagan attempted to implement a national health care plan. Only Reagan succeeded. His IMPALA Plan passed in 1986 gave everyone access to health care through our hospital emergency rooms. Unfortunately, funding was not part of the plan. Hospitals immediately felt the financial burden of caring for thousands of infirmed patients with no money to pay the bill.

Most of what has been tried to repair our health care system has failed. Perhaps Obamacare has come the closest to success though it was flawed from the beginning. It was created in 2008, partially passed in 2009, and completely implemented in 2014. The goal was to get 40 million people under some kind of insurance plan. It succeeded in reaching about 50 percent of that goal.

The worst thing about Obamacare as well as the more recent Republican solutions is that planning. One cannot hide 100 Senators behind closed doors and create a health care plan that will meet the necessities of our people. Planning with total involvement and total opportunities for input are the key.

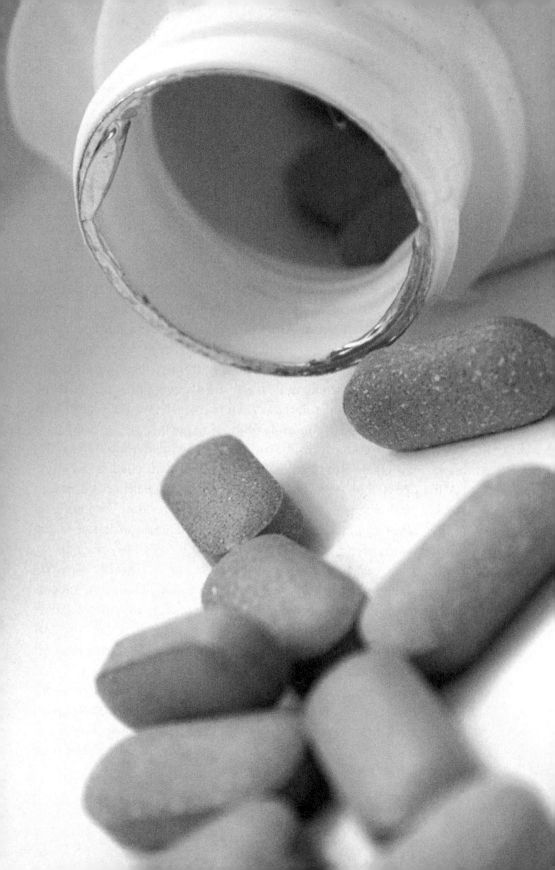

HEALTH CARE: WHAT IS THE SOLUTION?

The Affordable Health Care Law (Obamacare) is self-destructing. The new plan presented by the Republicans can't get enough votes to pass the Senate. It's a mess.

We have had four major efforts to deal with health care in the history of the United States. These include the creation of Social Security in 1936, Medicare and Medicaid in 1966, Reagan's IMPALA law in 1986, and President Obama's Affordable Health Care Law.

Reagan's IMPALA law was simple and easy to understand. It required hospitals to provide medical care for those who could not pay for it. **It is good to remember what the AHC plan was designed to accomplish.** It wasn't long until the bill for indigent care at most hospital exceeded 25% of the total budget, an impossible burden for local hospitals. Hospital leadership in the country called the situation untenable. Many smaller hospitals across the country closed. The American Hospital Association became a major support group for the passage of The Affordable Health Care Law, not necessarily because they liked it but because they needed to get out from under the burden of IMPALA.

Social Security and Medicare both were passed by Congress and then given an 18 month waiting period before becoming completely operational. The plan was to pass the measures as philosophy/concept and then for the healthcare industry and others directly involved to provide input and "hone" them into workable programs for the long term. Social Security has now been in force for 81 years and Medicare for more than 50. Neither is without their critics but, for the most part, both plans have worked to the benefit of the country.

What was true of Social Security and Medicare was planned for the Affordable Health Care Law. It was passed with some detail but, primarily, as philosophy/concept and then set up to have 18 months to work on the details. Unfortunately, one political party refused to work on the new law saying from the beginning that it should be repealed. Thus, unlike the Social Security and Medicare laws, it had very little done to it in the 18 month "dead" period prior to its full enactment in 2014.

It is good to remember what the AHC plan was designed to accomplish. At the time we had more than 40 million people in the country without health care insurance. The AHC was designed to get everyone under some kind of coverage.

Another negative is the fact that currently we have more than 180 million Americans on employer-provided health insurance. Explaining how health care became attached to business and industry would require us to retrace history to the days following WWII, an exercise for another time. Suffice it to say that because of such fringe benefits for U.S. workers, American business is at a major disadvantage attempting to compete in the world marketplace with businesses from countries that have government provided health care. Our international balance of payments, (sales versus purchases) has been negative since 1976. Count the number of foreign cars on our highways for proof.

Our healthcare system, actually a non-system, has been problematic for years. It grew to its present state with little united planning and virtually no comprehensive leadership.

How should we solve this problem? First, we need our best and brightest to work together to solve the nation's healthcare problem. Then, as is true in any planning model, we need to focus on "what:" what we want, what will work, what will best meet the needs of our people. Finally, we need comprehensive planning to create an approach that takes us from where we are to where we need to be.

We need a national commission to bring our healthcare professionals to one table with a mandate to give us what is needed to solve our dilemma. Can it be solved? Of course it can. Many other countries solved it years ago. Will everyone be happy with the outcome? Dream on.

HERE WE GO AGAIN ON HEALTH CARE

The Republican Health Care Plan was before Congress for about a week before it was withdrawn. Why? It just didn't have the votes to pass. It was opposed by both Democrats and a number of Republicans. So, back we go to square one.

We have been told since the passage of The Affordable Healthcare Act back in 2009 that the Republicans intended to replace that legislation with something much better. All of us, Republicans and Democrats, would appreciate having a comprehensive health care plan that meets the needs of our citizens. The experts tell us that the current plan has not solved the two big healthcare issues, which are access to services and containing costs. The latter is a key factor in our national debt as healthcare costs are approaching 20 percent of our nation's GDP.

The current plan has not solved the two big issues, which are access to services and containing costs.

Presidents who set out to reform health care include Truman, Kennedy, Nixon, Reagan, Clinton, Obama, and now Trump. Only President Reagan actually signed into law a measure that created universal health care for all. It was called The Emergency Medical Treatment and Labor Act (EMTALA-1986). The goal of that law was to make it illegal for hospitals to refuse care to those who could not pay for it. His law created a major burden on hospitals to fund the care of those uncovered by insurance. It solved one problem but created another.

Like our current law, the hastily put together plan offered by the Republicans was not the solution to our health care problems either. As should be obvious, neither Plan deals effectively with the key issues of access and cost.

The healthcare industry has many internal and external publics. In fact, every citizen is involved in the health care issue and most have opinions on how healthcare should be resolved.

President Trump said, "Nobody knew health care could be so complicated." At least six previous presidents knew. In fact, providing a comprehensive health care program for our citizens is one of the most complicated domestic problems ever faced by our country.

Who has a plan that will provide access at a reasonable cost? The current plan provides for access but a lack of cost containment is the single major item that is causing insurance companies to abandon participation.

The Affordable Healthcare Act was conceived behind closed doors by a Democratic Congress. Now, the Republicans have followed suit and have done the same thing with their proposed replacement. Do we really think that a group of lawyers (Congress) can produce a healthcare plan that is best for the country? I don't. We need to leave the defense of our country, the education of our children, and the health of our nation to the professionals with the training and experience to, "make it right."

Despite all good intentions, Congress is incapable of giving us what is needed. We should be pleased the Republican plan has been withdrawn. The purpose of Congress is not to be the architect of programs that are beyond the training and expertise of its membership. Instead, the role of Congress is to supervise from a distance while our system of supply and demand, checks and balances, adjusts itself to our nation's needs. The make-up of Congress is primarily citizens trained in the intricacies of law but not in complicated societal issues such as healthcare.

Who then can solve the healthcare problem for us? Healthcare isn't a Republican problem or a Democrat problem. It is a United States of America problem. We need a commission made up of professionals from the healthcare community to solve this problem. When it convenes every interest group within the field of healthcare should be represented and all "best" ideas should be heard. We need to focus our nation's resources on a solution and we need our best trained and most experienced minds to focus on the problem together. Partisan politics will not solve this problem.

10

SPECIAL DAYS

Most businesses recognize nine special days each year. But, nine is just the beginning. We start the year with New Year's Day and finish it with several days of celebration for the Christmas holidays. In between we celebrate Martin Luther King, Jr. Day, Valentine's Day, Easter, Mother and Father's days, Memorial and Labor Day, Independence Day, Veteran's Day, Thanksgiving, and Pearl Harbor Day. It sounds like that should be an exhaustive list but other special days such as Flag Day and VJ Day are not included. In short, we have lots of special days.

When Ruth and I spent a year in Sri Lanka working on a new college for the government there, we were surprised to find that they had more special days that anyplace we had ever heard of. It seems that when they broke away from Great Britain in the late 40s they wanted to create a country that was accepting of all creeds and cultures. They decided to accept all religious holidays of the major religions. So, they celebrate Ramadan, Christmas, Passover, Pentecost, Easter, as well as a series of Buddhist celebration days including The Enlightenment, Buddha's birthday, etc. Perhaps the strangest one was Poya, the day of the full moon. Since a full moon comes almost once each month, that is one day each month when no one works.

For many of us the calendar revolves around those special days. It is the time each year when families get together, when friends go out together to celebrate, when we all seem to draw closer to each other. We do covet those special times of celebration.

A VISIT TO THE PUNCH BOWL
ON PEARL HARBOR DAY

It's a short drive from Honolulu and Pearl Harbor up to the Punch Bowl, the Cemetery of the Pacific, where so many of our young people who fought in World War II, Korea, and Vietnam have been laid to rest. The cemetery is called the Punch Bowl because of its round shape and its setting in an extinct volcano. The view from the top of a mountain overlooking Honolulu and the Pacific Ocean is surely one of the more beautiful cemetery settings anyplace in the world.

> **We watched the bubbles of oil come up to the surface from the hulk of the Battleship, as it had for more than 60 years.**

Earlier in the day we had visited the Arizona Memorial in Pearl Harbor, had watched the bubbles of oil come up to the surface from the hulk of the Battleship, as it had for more than sixty years. It was as if someone below was signaling they were still there and wished to be rescued. Unfortunately, those men who were entombed below and those on the other ships sunk that fateful day on December 7th, 1941 would not be rescued and would not see their families again.

My host for the day was my brother, a career Naval officer. He and I took NROTC in College getting ready for service in the Navy. He made it through and I didn't. I was 4-F with a bad shoulder joint which would have passed the physical easily had we been involved in a war at the time. In his 20 years in the Navy, my brother had sailed on all of the seven seas and handled amphibious landings in Vietnam during the height of that war. He had watched bullet-riddled helicopters sitting down on deck with the arms and legs of the dead and wounded hanging out of the doorways. He could place a value on those lives that could not be understood by one who had not stood in jeopardy, willing to give the most valuable thing he had to give, his

life. Thankfully, my brother did not lose his life fighting our Nation's wars. He could be there to tell me and others why "war is hell" and that our country should avoid it except as a very last resort.

Pearl Harbor is one of our country's greatest tragedies but, also, is a symbol of our finest hour. It was there that we met a fierce enemy and, facing the real possibility of defeat, forged a resolution in our minds to never again be caught unprepared. We also resolved to revere forever the sacrifice of those who stood in our place, who fought for our country and our way of life. We shall never forget Pearl Harbor or those who are laid to rest there in the Punch Bowl.

CELEBRATING FLAG DAY

There are many stories written about our flag but none could rival the drama of Francis Scott Key's writing of the poem that became our National Anthem. It was about the battle for Ft. McHenry in Baltimore Harbor during the War of 1812. Our flag played a prominent role in the story he told.

Key was a young lawyer living in Georgetown just outside of Washington DC during that fateful time when the War of 1812 began. Earlier that year the British had sailed up the Potomac River, captured Washington DC, and burned the Capital and the White House. President Madison and his Cabinet barely escaped to a safer location.

Following the capture of Washington DC the British focused their attacks on the neighboring city of Baltimore. Word reached Francis Scott Key that a much loved physician, Dr. William Beanes, had been carried off by the British. They were holding him on the British flagship, Tonnant, and there was great fear that the British would hang the elder doctor. The townspeople asked the young attorney for his help in negotiating Dr. Beanes' release.

The silence could mean only one thing. The battle was over. But did the fort fall to the British or was it still standing?

Key and a friend, John Skinner, went to the Tonnant under a flag of truce and secured the release of the beloved Doctor. However, the British, then engaged in an attack on Ft. McHenry, forced them to stay on board the British ship while the battle raged through the night.

The attack on the fort continued for 25 hours. The night sky seemed ablazewith rockets flying through the air and bombs bursting in the distance across the walls of the fort. Key and Skinner knew that as long as the night sky was lit up and the sounds of explosions filled the air, the fort had not surrendered.

Being an amateur poet, Key began to write. With the motivation of the battle raging in the distance and the growing anxiety about the fate of the fort and the soldiers inside, the verses poured out of him. Finally, in the predawn darkness, the rockets stopped and the sound of the exploding bombs faded away. The silence could mean only one thing, the battle was over. But, did the fort fall to the British or was it still standing?

Key and Skinner stood at the ships rail and strained in the darkness to see across the ramparts if the flag of their fledgling country was still flying. Finally, as dawn began to break they could make out the movement of the flag with the stars and stripes waving in the wind. That flag would someday be called Old Glory, The Grand Old Flag, The Star Spangled Banner, and many other titles of reverence and admiration.

Key's poetic inspiration continued as the boat took the three, Key, Skinner, and Dr. Beane, back to shore. He finished his last line in a hotel later in the day and the rest is history. The next time you sing the words to that hallowed anthem remember its context and see if the words have new meaning for you.

Key's poem, titled "The Defense of Fort McHenry", appeared in newspapers as far away as Georgia and New Hampshire. Not long after the poem was first published Ferdinand Durang, a stage actor in Baltimore, applied the tune of a song of the time entitled, "Anacreon in Heaven" to the poem. In its first public presentation as a song he gave it the name, "The Star Spangled Banner".

The song was a favorite for civic and military occasions for a hundred years until, in 1931, it was adopted by Congress as our National Anthem.

Francis Scott Key's original poem had eight sections each with four lines. We won't reprint all of it here but the last section is worthy of note when one considers the United States of America in the 21st Century.

Then conquer we must, when our cause it is just,
and this be our motto: "In God is our trust"
and the star-spangled banner in triumph shall wave
O'er the land of the free and the home of the brave.

CONSIDER THE TURKEY

Ruth and I were driving through the Smoky Mountains last weekend and came upon a gaggle of turkeys on the side of the road. A few weeks ago the same thing happened while we were on the way to Due West. It makes one wonder what the turkey population might have been two hundred years ago before this area was settled and South Carolina didn't have almost five million people.

We are approaching Thanksgiving Day, 2015, a day often referred to as Turkey-Day. It is an American tradition that one of the items on the dinner table at Thanksgiving will be turkey. It has been that way since that first Thanksgiving celebrated by the Puritans in New England almost 500 years ago.

President Abraham Lincoln started a new tradition in 1865 when he "pardoned" the White House turkey. Every president since then has had a ceremony at Thanksgiving where the White House turkey was pardoned. The pardoned turkeys have traditionally been given to the George Washington home of Mount Vernon located on the Potomac just south of Washington, DC. The one

Abraham Lincoln started a new tradition when he pardoned the White House turkey.

exception to that custom might have been during the presidency of Harry Truman. Truman held the traditional pardoning ceremony but, oddly, no turkeys showed up at Mr. Vernon. No one really knows what happened to the Truman turkeys. Knowing the reputation of the always practical and pragmatic Truman, I suspect I can make a good guess.

During our nation's formative years, Benjamin Franklin

proposed the Turkey as our national bird. He reasoned that it had fed a high percentage of our settlers and frontiersmen during our early years and deserved serious consideration because it was such a consistent source of food. John Adams countered with the Eagle as our national bird. Franklin pointed out that the Eagle was primarily a scavenger that lived off of the carcasses of other animals. Adams responded that the Turkey had to be the dumbest bird God every created. Franklin said the Eagle had only one thing to recommend it and that was that Indians liked its feathers. John Adams supposedly ended the conversation with the admonition to Franklin that, "Ben, our national bird just can't be a turkey." Thank goodness for John Adams' ability to win an argument or we might still be saluting a turkey.

I have one memory that re-appears every Thanksgiving. One year when I was about eight years old I remember being at the children's table with my brother and our cousins. Everyone had a plate but me. I was looking around wondering why I had been left out when my grandmother arrived with my plate. When she sat it down in front of me it held the largest turkey drumstick anyone ever saw. I'm sure my eyes were as big as saucers. I must have looked like that kid in the Norman Rockwell painting depicting Thanksgiving.

D-DAY: ONE OF HISTORY'S "FLY THE FLAG" DAYS

June 6th, is a "fly the flag" day for all who can remember the majesty and tragedy of The Normandy Invasion. That was the day when almost 200,000 soldiers, about half of them American, stormed Normandy Beach on the northern coast of France in the greatest amphibious assault in the history of warfare.

Prior to that date the U.S. and its allies were fighting an up-hill battle from the deserts of northern Africa to the beaches of Dunkirk. England had been under siege from the air by German rockets. Ships at sea were constantly harassed by U-boat attacks as Germany attempted to sever the supply lines that supported our troops.

It was an unusual family in the United States that did not have a member in service somewhere overseas. More than 3 million of our men and women were in uniform and those who weren't were working to support the war effort. Every resource, every bit of brain power, every emotion was devoted to winning the war because defeat, bowing to the Nazi war machine, was simply unthinkable.

Every resource, every bit of brain power, every emotion was devoted to winning the war.

Dwight Eisenhower was our European Theatre of Operations General. He was in that role not because he was a master battle tactician but, instead, because he was a genius at the logistics of supplying the war machine. Perhaps more importantly, he was highly skilled at handling the massive egos of our allies Joseph Stalin of Russia, Winston Churchill of England,

Charles DE Gaulle of France and the top Generals, Montgomery of England and Patten of the U.S., whose capabilities on the battlefield were so important to ultimate victory. Eisenhower's calm voice and soft handed approach were exactly what was needed. He was able to guide all of the personalities into a unified fighting force that could take on the Axis powers that had conquered northern Africa and most of Europe by the mid-1940s.

Planning for the invasion had begun a full two years before but the actual date was decided by, wouldn't you know it, the weather. Altogether, more than 9000 ships and 340,000 men and women were involved in the assault. Within seven days there were more than 425,000 dead, wounded, or missing from both sides. The massive cemeteries of Normandy remind us of their sacrifice.

The Normandy Invasion was the "watershed" event of WWII. Prior to June 6th, 1944 the U.S. and its allies were in a defensive struggle. After the successful beach head on the northern coast of France all of our forces were in an attack mode, with every thrust focused on shutting down the Nazi war machine and gaining unconditional surrender.

June 6th is a "fly the flag" day. Lets show our colors on June 6th to honor that great occasion.

HAVE YOU FOUND YOUR
CHRISTMAS SPIRIT YET?

The Christmas season is here again. How's your Christmas spirit? More to the point, what is it that kindles your Christmas spirit?

I have to admit that my Christmas spirit is more difficult to kindle this year than in previous years. I am now at what one might call "superior vintage," and because I am older I am losing friends almost every Year. This year has been a difficult year for losing friends. With every loss comes a feeling of nostalgia, accompanied by floods of memories of those very close and important relationships, some from as far back as childhood. Much of that is good but it creates a feeling of loss never-the-less. Friends and family are what make the world a place of joy and love and that should be emphasized to us with every Christmas season.

We often go looking for our Christmas spirit at Dollywood in Pigeon Forge.

Ruth and I often go looking for our Christmas spirit at Dollywood in Pigeon Forge, Tennessee but haven't been able to squeeze that into our schedule yet this year. We may get there yet. We still have three weeks. But, we both agree that we need something to get us revved up and thinking "right". The Dollywood Christmas shows always get us headed in the right direction. Any excuse to go to Dollywood this time of year is good enough for us. We do enjoy that place with all of its performing young people, its beautiful lights, and Christmas music playing on every corner.

Music is a major factor in any Christmas season. Whether it is "Here Comes Santa Claus", "White Christmas", or "Rudolph" it begins to dominate your psyche. The music that really closes the deal are "Hark the Harold Angels sing," "Away in a Manger", and "O Little Town of Bethlehem". A night of listening to Carols by Candlelight at one or another of the churches in the area always seem to be just what the doctor ordered. We love the singing Christmas trees and the annual Christmas parade.

The spirit of Christmas culminates each year with church Christmas programs. The singing of little children and church choirs tell us each year of that wonderful story of a babe lying in a manger with shepherds and wise men kneeling at his feet, of families gathering to renew the bond that was kindled in all of those Christmases past.

I can remember a succession of great aunts coming to visit at my grandmother's house when I was a boy,—Aunt Nora, Aunt Goldie, Aunt Pearl, Aunt Philomena, and Aunt Lela. (Don't you just love those names from the 19th Century?) All of these dear ladies are gone now but their faces are still as crystal clear to me as they were a generation ago. Each would arrive with her tray of divinity, fudge, brownies, and my favorite of favorites, chocolate chip cookies. Is it any wonder that I can close my eyes today and still smell the wonderful kitchen fragrance that filled the house each year at Christmas time? Is it any wonder I still spend several hours a week at the "Y" doing battle with the bulges created by the remnants of all those wonderful memories?

Such memories get us ready for the big day, the day we welcome friends and family to our homes as the Holy family did when the shepherds arrived to "see this miraculous thing," when we open the presents just as the Holy family did 2000 years ago with the visit of the Magi, when we focus on the blessed Christ child who is, lest we forget, the reason for the season.

So we wish for you a growing Christmas spirit that will stay with you all year round, and a wonderful Christmas season with your family and friends.

SHARING THE CHRISTMAS STORY:
ENGLAND AND THE KING JAMES BIBLE

Rejoice, prophecy is fulfilled, Jesus is born, the long awaited Messiah has come. How do we know? The Bible tells us so. Research tells us that the United States is a country where most believe in a supreme being. We owe that belief to the King James Bible whose 405th birthday we celebrate this year. Yes, there have been other revisions of the Bible in recent years but the foundation of it all is that English translation of the Bible created in England in 1611 A.D.

The Bible's impact on our lives necessitates knowing how it came into existence.

During this season of the year we acknowledge the birth of the Christ child whose story is told in the Books of Matthew and Luke in the King James Bible. That book's impact on our lives necessitates knowing how that Bible came into existence.

In 1611 England was a small island kingdom in the north Atlantic with a population of less than one million. Over the next 300 years England created an empire that stretched around the globe. It was said that "the sun never sets on the British Empire."

The man, James 1st of England, was as unlikely a religious leader as England was an unlikely world power. He was a Scott and not English by birth and was raised as a Catholic. His mother, Queen Mary of Scotland, was a second cousin to Queen Elizabeth of England. When Elizabeth died she left no heir. To fill her vacant throne the English leadership looked for her oldest male relative and found James, who was then King of Scotland. He became the King of England and ruled both countries from London.

King James found England to be a country with an almost equal Catholic-Protestant population and a religious split so great that violence often erupted between the religious groups. Churches, both Catholic and Protestant, were burned and Priests and Ministers were killed.

After a thorough study of the situation King James decided to try to bring the two warring factions together by creating a common Bible to be used by both Catholics and Protestants. It took months of wide ranging discussions, disagreements, and compromise but the new Bible came into being. Peace did not come immediately between the religious factions but the plan began to work and things were better.

Prior to this time in history, Spain had been the dominate force in the world. They had gained great wealth with their discovery and exploration of the new world. England was coming late to challenge Spain on the high seas. With the war between Spain and England that ended with the English defeat of the Spanish Armada in 1588, England stepped forward to become the new leader in the world. As luck, or God's plan, would have it, shortly following the conflict with Spain the new Bible was being made ready to share with the world.

As England planted their flag all around the globe, they took along their English language, their culture, and their King James Bible. Soon, the result of King James' efforts to solve the religious divisions of England began to be felt around the world in all British territories.

For those of us who believe that "God works in mysterious ways his wonders to perform," there is no happenstance. The creation of the King James Bible was both planned and ordained as was England's rise to world leadership that gave them the opportunity to share their Bible around the globe.

As you celebrate the Christmas season with your family this year give a thought to King James I of England and the Bible he created that has enabled all of us to know the story of Christmas.

*** *Reference: The book God's Secretaries.*

PRESENTS OR PRESENCE

We have just passed through another "black" Friday. It is that one day after Thanksgiving when the stores at the malls open at six A.M. and stay open until mid-night. It's black Friday because retail merchants expect their labors over the past year to finally get out of the "red" and into the black, when the monthly ledger will finally show a positive balance. On that day each year I stay out of the stores and I hesitate to even drive by the mall on the way to anywhere.

Perhaps it was the Three Wise Men who started all the trouble. They brought presents with them when they followed the star to Bethlehem to see the baby Jesus. Ever since, we have been giving presents to each other to celebrate Christmas. To be fair, people in many cultures and religions find excuses to give gifts, much to the joy of the recipients and the store owners.

> **Perhaps it was the Three Wise Men who started all the trouble.**

In the Christmas story, the Three Wise Men brought gold, frankincense and myrrh. Gold is still very acceptable, frankincense and myrrh less so. (For one thing, those items are hard to find at Wal-Mart.) If the three kings of the Orient had been as wise as advertised they might have brought a broom to the stable. (By the time they arrived in Bethlehem the scriptures tell us the little family had moved into a house.)

One of the realities of growing older is that there comes a time when you don't feel the need for more presents. When you were young, Santa could gift wrap a brick and make you happy. All of us with children can remember when, by the afternoon of Christmas Day, children were playing more with boxes the toys came in than with the toys.

Sadly, the excitement of a Christmas present slowly wanes as the years go by. Sure, it is always nice to receive a sweater, a tie or socks. These are useful gifts and reassuring tokens that somebody cares. But, year after year, something that might be called sweater fatigue sets in. It is probably a sign of being spoiled but, after a while, it's hard to clap hands and say, "Oh my, a sweater!"

Every family has a Scrooge who never got a present he didn't already have two of and, if he didn't, this one was certainly the wrong color. Sweater fatigue. Socks fatigue. Underwear fatigue. You can make up your own name for it. By a certain age, it isn't presents you need from those who love you. What you need is presence, the presence of those we love and of those who love us.

Perhaps the Wise Men knew this. It wasn't the gold, frankincense and myrrh that were important. It was simply their presence for the adoration of the Christ child. After all, they had traveled half way across the mid-east to "see this thing that had come to pass." That isn't exactly "over the river and through the woods, to grandmother's house," but whatever distance it was, it made such an impact that we are still reading about it two thousand years later.

The commercialism of Christmas is something that is lamented from church pulpits on Christmas Sunday. Commercialism is our blessing and our curse. Too often, the promise of peace on Earth and goodwill among men seems to have been postponed until further notice. But we can do something about that by following the highest star of the human heart.

What I want for Christmas is for the lonely to be visited, neglected parents to be loved, and distant relatives to be called or, better yet, invited. Personally, all I want for Christmas is to be with my family, all of my family, every one of them. Presents are fine, presence is better.

Ruth and I wish you all a wonderful Christmas with lots of presence and, yes, some presents too.

WE CAN BE TRULY THANKFUL

My son and his family moved to Providence, RI several years ago and our visits there have caused me to review several facts of history related to our traditional first Thanksgiving in Massachusetts.

There were only 102 colonists at Plymouth in 1621 and without the help of the local Indian tribe, the Wanpanoags, more than half would have starved. The local Indians showed the colonists how to raise corn and how to fish the local waters around Plymouth Bay.

Abraham Lincoln was the first President to designate a national day of thanksgiving.

Tradition tells us the first Thanksgiving celebration occurred in present day Massachusetts. However, St. Augustine, Florida says the Spanish had such a celebration in the late 1500s and the history of the colony of Jamestown in present day Virginia says they had a Thanksgiving service in 1609. Who was first? Who cares? The important thing is that we acknowledge we have much to be thankful for and set aside a day every year for a day devoted to thanksgiving. Abraham Lincoln was the first President to designate a national day of thanksgiving and Franklin D. Roosevelt designated the third Thursday in November to be the annual day.

The detailed history of that time tells us that the colonists decided to have a day of thanksgiving and to invite their benefactors, the Wanpanoags. Captain Miles Standish and local councilman Stephen Hopkins were dispatched to the closest Wanpanoag village to make the invitation. They had some difficulty making their Indian friends understand what they were offering but, eventually, they made themselves understood. The appointed day arrived and as we often say, "A good time was had by all."

In 2011 celebrating comes a little hard for some of our fellow citizens. Unemployment is at 9.1% and even deducting the hard core unemployed numbers from that group we still have more than five million people who want to work but can't find jobs. Unemployment

compensation, though extended twice, is still running out for many and house payments and the purchase of other necessities gets more and more problematical.

On the positive side, everyone is aware of the problem and in America when a serious problem is identified and we get focused on finding a solution we generally find one. When we had the problem in the 30's, the 50's, and the 80's we found a solution.

In the meantime we can celebrate that 91 percent of those who want jobs have them and, despite tales of woe with Fannie Mae and Freddie Mac, 92 percent of mortgages are being paid on time.

WHEN CHRISTMAS MUSIC COMES ALIVE

Several years back I spend most of December in India visiting several cities. It was the 22nd of December when I was on a plane moving down the taxiway headed for home. Just at the edge of my consciousness I became aware that the wonderful Christmas Carol "Hark, the Herald Angeles Sing" was playing on the intercom. It had been a year since I had heard Christmas music and I had not been thinking about Christmas at all since the normal decorations of the season are not generally found in most parts of India. Suddenly, the feeling of heading for home, of family and Christmas, was very much on my mind and I closed my eyes to listen to a song about Angels and a new born King. There was an emotion that swept over me that is difficult to describe.

Let us bend our knee with shepherds and wise men.

C.S. Lewis said, "If we find ourselves with a desire that nothing in this world can satisfy, the most probable explanation is that we were made for another world." Yet, we need a Savior to show us the way to that other world, the same one promised by the prophets of old. They said, "O Come, O Come, Emmanuel", "Come thou long expected Jesus."

Those prayers were answered at the first Christmas when "It Came upon the Midnight Clear", in "O Little Town of Bethlehem", where in the stillness of that "Silent Night, Holy Night", they found that Messiah, "Away in a Manger." Those "Angels from the Realms of Glory" sang the first Christmas carols that night and proclaimed astonishing news, "Hark, the Herald Angels Sing", "Glory to the New Born King." Their song was an invitation to worship and they told us, "O Come, All Ye Faithful," and in their song the angels answered the most important question ever asked, "What Child is this?"

He is both "Infant Holy, Infant Lowly", the son of God, but who came to earth to take on human flesh. So, "Joy to the World! The Lord is Come", "Good Christian Men, Rejoice" because he came to

save us from ourselves. Those who believe in the Christ of Christmas will find an answer for their longing hearts. "God Rest You Merry, Gentlemen". This news is too good to keep to one's self, so proclaim it to all the earth. "Go, tell it on the Mountain."

Each Christmas season, we celebrate the birth of our Savior in song. We joy in singing the old carols in worship and join with the Angelic choir. Let us bend our knee with shepherds and wise men. Because, "On Christmas Night All Christians Sing," "Glory to the New Born King."

ALWAYS DREAMING
OF A WHITE CHRISTMAS

My favorite secular Christmas song of all time is "I'm Dreaming of a White Christmas". I love the simplicity of the lyrics and the mental visions it creates such as snow glistening on treetops and Christmas cards being written. Having been raised in the mid-west and now living in the south, the wistful dream of a White Christmas captures me.

The song was written by Irvin Berlin in 1940 but it didn't really hit the public's consciousness until Bing Crosby sang it in the hit movie "White Christmas" in 1954. The song has sold more than 50 million copies since and is the most successful record of all time.

Bing Crosby didn't particularly like the song when he first heard it.

Bing Crosby said that he didn't particularly like the song when he first heard it and was not scheduled to sing it in the movie. The "White Christmas" director, Michael Curtiz, wrote in his memoirs that he intended for Crosby to sing it but Crosby insisted he wouldn't be in the movie if he had to sing that song. It wasn't until they were nearing the completion of filming that they sprung it on Crosby. As the story goes, he refused to come to the set for two days after learning he had been duped but, eventually, relented and sang the song. The rest, as they say, is history.

Most of the movie stars of the 30s and 40s were graduates of Vaudeville, that stage show circuit that ran from Boston, to Buffalo to Philadelphia to Baltimore and, finally, if the act was good enough, to New York. Names like W.C. Fields, Mae West, Bob Hope, Jack Benny, Bing Crosby, and Irving Berlin were well known in the theatres of the 36 Vaudeville circuit cities, all of them in the snowy northeast.

When movies began to be made with sound, song writers like Irvin Berlin and singers like Bing Crosby found their way to

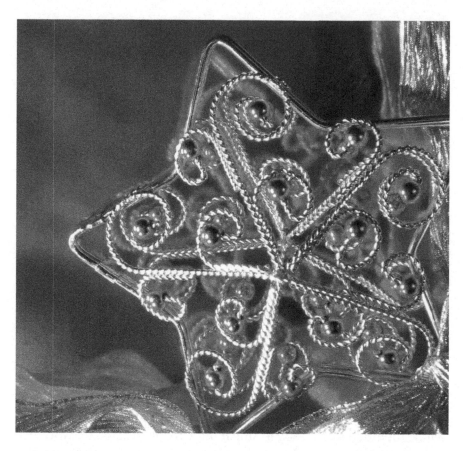

California. There, of course, Christmas was very different from what most of the Vaudevillians were used to. You could understand their longing for a white Christmas. The original words to Berlin's classic, long lost today, were.......".The sun is shining, the grass is green, the orange and palm trees sway. There's never been such a day in Beverly Hills, L.A. But, it's December twenty-fourth and I'm longing to be up North"....... Then, the chorus began with the familiar words, "I'm dreaming of a White Christmas."

Ruth and I have lived in South Carolina now for more than 30 years and, though we have had some snow from time to time, we have not yet experienced a white Christmas. So, assuming it won't happen this year either, Ruth and I have a wish for you..."May your days be merry and bright, even if your Christmas can't be white."

WINSTON CHURCHILL: A GREAT AMERICAN

November 30th is the birthday of Winston Churchill, one of our greatest Americans. Wait a minute. Wasn't he Prime Minister of England during the Second World War? Yes, that is true. However, Winston Churchill was the son of Jeanette "Jenny" Jerome, who was born in the Cobble Hill section of Brooklyn, NY in 1854 when Brooklyn was still a separate city, and he was given honorary American citizenship by an act of Congress in 1963. So, by birth and by an act of Congress he is as American as any of us. Certainly, he was one of the greatest leaders and personalities of the 20th century and he had the spirit, drive, and determination to which all of us should aspire.

He also was one of the greatest inspirational speakers of all time, the kind who could lift the emotions of listeners and motivate them to do what was necessary and what was right. We could use him today in the U.S. Congress or in the pulpits of America. Listen to some of his words.

On History: "A nation that forgets its past has no future."

On Politics: "You have enemies? Good. That means you've stood up for something in your life."

On Americans: "You can always count on Americans to do the right thing—after they've tried everything else."

On Diplomacy: Diplomacy is the art of telling people to go to hell in such a way that they ask for directions."

On Optimism: "A pessimist sees the difficulty in every opportunity; An optimist sees the opportunity in every difficulty."

On Courage: "Fear is a reaction. Courage is a decision."

On Conviction: "One man with conviction will overwhelm a hundred who have only opinions."

On Democracy: "It has been said that democracy is the worst form of government except all the others that have been tried." "The best argument against democracy is a five-minute conversation with the average voter."

On Cigars: "Smoking cigars is like falling in love. First you are attracted to its shape. You stay with it for its flavor. And you must always remember never, never let the flame go out.

Exchanges with others: With Bessie Braddock: "Sir, you are drunk." "Yes, I am, but you are ugly. In the morning I shall be sober." With Nancy Astor: "Sir, if you were my husband, I would give you poison." "Lady Astor, if I were your husband I would take it." On Clement Atlee: "He is a modest man, who has much to be modest about."

On an appeaser: One who feeds the crocodile hoping it will eat him last.

On the war effort: "We shall fight on the beaches, we shall fight on the landing grounds, we shall fight in the fields and in the streets, we shall fight in the hills; we shall never surrender." "What is our aim? I can answer with one word: Victory—victory at all costs, victory in spite of all terror, victory however long and hard the road may be." "Let us, therefore, brace ourselves to our duties, and so bear ourselves that, if the British Empire and its Commonwealth lasts for a thousand years, men will still say, 'This was their finest hour'!"

On life: What is the use of living, if not to strive for nobler causes and to make this world a better place for those who will live in it after we are gone?'

If memories of WW II have faded, the new movie, Dunkirk, reminds us of when the world was in jeopardy from Nazi Germany and Winston Churchill was the voice of defiance in Europe. He stood as the symbol of resistance in England and waited for the belated entry of the United States into the war that preserved our way of life.

Happy Birthday, Mr. Churchill. When you stood toe to toe with Hitler, you may have saved us all.

WORDS THAT CHANGED THE WORLD

When the signing of the Declaration of Independence was announced on the 4th of July in 1776 it set off the greatest display of fireworks in the history of the world. No, they were not the exploding, fill the skies, fireworks we use to celebrate on the 4th of July today. They were the fireworks generated by the spirit of freedom and by the desires of free thinking people everywhere to breathe the air of self-determination.

Today, amid questions about the content of our Constitution and the wording of various phrases and clauses which have shaped our lives, we still stand amazed at the foresight of our Founding Fathers, the creators of the Declaration of Independence, The Constitution, and The Bill of Rights. Those three documents were written by some of the greatest minds in the history of the world.

> **We still stand amazed at the foresight of our Founding Fathers, the creators of the Declaration of Independence.**

Thomas Jefferson wrote the lines that opened the Declaration of Independence and with those words affected the lives of millions of people all over the globe. Let's look more closely at the beginning of that great document.

We hold these truths to be self evident, that all men are created equal, that they are endowed by the Creator with certain unalienable rights, that among these are Life, Liberty, and the pursuit of Happiness. That to secure these rights, Governments are instituted among men deriving their just powers from the consent of the governed.

At that time in history no government had ever been established on the principle that men were created equal. Further, the only "rights" known to the people and governments of Europe were "The Divine Right of Kings". It meant that God placed Kings in their positions and because that was true, the Kings could do no wrong.

They were God's chosen representatives on earth and were to be followed without question. It took the words of the Declaration of Independence to state in written form what was in the hearts of men everywhere, that we all deserved equal rights and that ..... among these rights were Life, Liberty, and the pursuit of Happiness.

The signers of the Declaration of Independence, hero's in American history, were all judged to be traitors by King George in England. After the signing, Benjamin Franklin was heard to say, "We had all better hang together or, most assuredly, we will all hang separately".

Who were these colonist who came together to create this amazing document that separated us from our Mother Country in Europe? They were names from our history like Hancock, Jefferson, Adams, Franklin, Calhoun and Family pride prompts me to mention Stephen Hopkins of Rhode Island. These were men of property, wealth, and prestige. They had much to lose. Every other revolution recorded in history, the French Revolution, Russian Revolution, etc. was led by desperate people fighting poverty and political repression. The foot soldiers of those revolutions were the poor, the disenfranchised, and the outcasts of society.

What was it that motivated our Founding Fathers to run such a risk? For all practical purposes, this group of leaders had little to gain and everything to lose. Yet, they took on the greatest military force the world had known up to that time and bet their very lives on victory. What possible motivation could make them do such a thing?

The answer is that they did it to be free, and they did it to make the rest of their nation, the poor, the disenfranchised, the outcasts, free as well. They did it so that their children and their children's children could live in a free society, the likes of which the world had never seen. They could look into the crystal ball of their vision for the future and see
a government that would value every person as an equal, that would allow each person to contribute what was uniquely theirs to contribute, and that government would not weigh more than the people could carry.

The U.S. Constitution that grew out of Jefferson's Declaration of Independence is less than a quarter of the length of the owner's manual for a new automobile, yet it provided the foundation for a new type of government that values freedom and individual rights.

That Constitution has provided stability for the most passionate, energetic, and inventive people in the history of the world. We Americans are, indeed, a strange group here in this melting pot that mixes colors, creeds, languages, and amazingly unique abilities. With all of our differences, it is the Constitution that is the great leveler, the document that makes us all equal before the law. Some very smart people disagree with parts of that document and want to make some changes, but I'm not for touching one comma of it.

The foundation truth of that document, of our society, of our freedoms is that the people must be trusted. We have fought wars and lost our fathers, husbands, brothers, daughters, and sons because we trust the people. Trust the people, trust them to do the right thing, trust them with freedom. Let the government help where it can, but trust the people. Lincoln said it best in the last few words of his Gettysburg Address....... "that this nation, under God, shall have a new birth of freedom, and that government of the people, by the people, for the people, shall not perish from the earth."

11

SPORTS

According to a recent reader's poll, seventy percent of the men who read a newspaper turn first to the sports pages. More than one hundred million viewers tuned in to watch the Super Bowl last week. If you decided to attend the game in person, tickets were selling on E-bay for just less than $4,000. Major League Baseball offers almost 5,000 games each year at an average cost of close to $80 per ticket. With an average attendance of 25,000 across all thirty teams, baseball fans are paying more than 600 million dollars to see professional baseball each year.

Some of our friends in Europe call the United States a "sports" society. There is more than ample evidence they are right. We have professional leagues in football, baseball, basketball, hockey, soccer, tennis, golf and, believe it or not, ping-pong. The list of college level sports in most major universities includes these and a dozen more. Then, there is high school, junior high, and even Little League and Pee Wee sports available in most communities.

Did I watch the Super Bowl last week? Oh, yes. Do I follow a college team? For sure. Did I play sports in younger years. No. Well, not unless you include football, basketball, baseball, tennis, golf and, well, you get the idea.

Early in my teaching career I was a junior high history teacher who was given the assignment of coaching the high school girl's volleyball team. We were back at the edge of the Ozarks and my anticipation of people who might turn out to see a volleyball game between two girl's teams was definitely slim and none. The night of the first game arrived and the gym started to fill up at five thirty. By game time we had every seat in the house filled with people sitting on the stage down on one end of the gym. It seems I greatly under

estimated the interest of the town's folk on a Friday night in a small town with little else going on.

Yes, we are a sports society. Then, any self-respecting columnist should write about sports, shouldn't he? So, read on. You may be surprised at what you read.

CLEMSON, GEORGIA, AND ANDERSON COLLEGE

Yes, Anderson College. The year was 1982, the last time prior to this past weekend that Clemson and Georgia football teams opened the season faced off together as a couple of nationally ranked teams.

Ruth and I had just moved to Anderson to become a part of Anderson College. At the time AC, as it was affectionately known in the community, was a small, 800 student, junior college known for its quality academic program and its men and women's basketball programs. Students were attracted to AC because of its size, Baptist background, and close proximity to Clemson.

It was my bright idea to invite students down to the president's house to see the game.

Many students who began college at Anderson finished at Clemson four years later. Most of the students bled orange and spent their days at AC but their weekends at Clemson involved in the many activities available there.

When Ruth and I came to Anderson we did not know we were moving to the center of the college sports world. It had escaped us that Georgia and Clemson had both won national football championships just prior to our coming, Georgia in 1980 and Clemson in 1981.

That weekend half or more of the students at AC had gone home and the dorms were less than half full. It was my bright idea to dial up the Clemson-Georgia game and invite students down to the President's home to see the game. We had not yet entered the era of the fifty inch TVs, I-Pads, and TV-phones. To prepare, we stocked up on soft drinks, set up a pop-corn machine on the back porch, and collected a supply of potato chips. We were expecting about 20 students. We had no idea the numbers that would respond.

Suffice it to say we were introduced to the rabid element of southern football fans almost immediately. The doorbell began to ring about two hours before game time. All of the food and drinks were exhausted before the game even began. We kept a steady stream of cars going back and forth to the supermarkets as the house filled up with students over and over. The consul TV in the large 20 X 50 family room became three TVs so everyone could see and the floor was so full of students that you could hardly move from one side of the room to the other. At one point I counted close to one hundred students and others were coming and going all through the game.

Students had arrived wearing their colors, about two-thirds in Orange and the rest in Red and Black. The noise after every play lifted the ceiling and various team yells were heard periodically through the evening.

Much has changed at AC over the past thirty years. It is now one of the top 100 private universities in the country with more than 3000 students. One thing that hasn't changed is the rabid football fans spawned in this area of the country, and the fact that teenagers can still eat the cupboards bare in a very short time.

COLLEGE FOOTBALL SEASON IS HERE

Once each year I indulge myself with an article on college football, one of my many passions. Here we are just a couple of weeks before the start of the college football season and the air waves are full of it. So, I am setting aside this space to share some thoughts on the subject.

Watching college football each year is wonderful and exciting. When my team wins it is beyond exciting. When they don't it is terribly deflating for the faithful fans. That is the way it is with sports. For every winner there is a loser. We just don't want our team to be on the losing end of the score.......ever. When they win we celebrate. When they lose we, well, just listen to the radio sports shows.

Despite being a lifetime fan, there are things about the sports world I can't figure out. For instance, when the team doesn't win why does everyone think they know the solution to the problem, whatever the problem is?

For every winner there is a loser. We just don't want our team to be on the losing end of the score ... ever.

If we didn't score enough it is because we didn't throw the ball or run the ball well enough, or we called the wrong plays. If we allowed the opposition to score it is because we didn't tackle well enough, we didn't dominate the line of scrimmage, or our defense was on the field too long and they were tired. I've always wondered about that last one. So, our defense is on the field a long time. Isn't the opposition's offense on the field the same length of time as our defense? Shouldn't they be as tired as our defense? What am I missing?

If our team's problems are so obvious wouldn't you think the coaches (we have several) would have figured it out by now?

Why does the university administration and local radio show managers think that former all-back-yard players make the best sportscasters? Many universities have training programs for sports broadcasters and they teach them how to properly communicate. Unfortunately, most don't.

When the game announcers call a game for the listening public why do they use terms such as "cover two" or "trips" in describing the play? "The defense is in cover two." "The offense is in trips to the right." If their purpose is to create a mental picture of what is happening on the field what kind of picture does "cover two" or "trips" give to the average listener. I assume that someone who has played college football will know what they are talking about. What percentage of the listening public do you suppose have played college football?

Having stated just a few concerns, I'm sure these problems will be solved as we move into this new football season. The university administrations all over the country read this column, don't they?

FOOTBALL HAS BECOME
OUR NATIONAL SPORT

It is almost that time of year when the fanatic football fan can be lost in the tumult of college and professional football. Husbands say goodbye to their wives, teenagers wear jerseys with favorite numbers on them, male and female alike begin to bleed orange, or blue, or red and black or whatever their favorite team's color is. Corporate America has a lucrative place to advertise, colleges invite their big donors to sit in the president's box, and Joe average gets his set of one hundred dollar tickets and begins his trek to row 72 on the sunny side of the stadium.

Medical research casts a shadow over the entire structure of football.

Football is played at the professional, college, high school, junior high, and even Pee-Wee levels. At every level coaches are reliving their glory days through their willing charges and young people are having a great time winning one for old Sywash. All the time we are watching this unfold, we are watching the mental health of our youth unravel. Statistics tell us that 89% of former professional football players have Chronic Traumatic Encephalophy (CTE) and many cannot remember their friends and family from day to day. Unfortunately, we have learned over the years that the best predictor of the future is the past, and the past results of football are devastating.

Yes, I know. Now I have begun to meddle. Football has become our national game. High school, college, and NFL stadiums are filled each weekend through the fall and those who don't attend are generally glued to their TV sets. Yet, medical research casts a shadow over the entire structure of football as it is played at all levels. Each fall we read again about the brain injuries of professional football players. The National Football League admitted responsibility for past head injuries to a level of more than 765 million dollars. And, there are only about 2000 active NFL players on 32 teams.

The problem at lower levels dwarfs the liability admitted by the NFL. There are more than 70,000 college players on approximately 1500 teams in the U.S. and the number of high school, junior high, and youth teams are impossible to count. Tragically, the research shows the younger the brain the more susceptible it is to injury. Suffice it to say that the number of young people we have involved in school and college sanctioned jeopardy is in the millions. The potential financial cost of such jeopardy may well be into the trillions. And, who can measure the human tragedy of a non-functioning brain.

Worse, we know the problem exists because of the published research and still we continue to create opportunities for brain mayhem at younger and younger ages. We trust coaches who are well schooled in the fundamentals of the sport. They spend, literally, years learning how to move a football down the field. Unfortunately, most high school and college coaches will admit to having no more than one or two courses that teach them how to protect the health of the young people in their charge. And, youth coaches? What orientation/training program gets them ready to handle possible concussion problems? Just as bad, the technology of the equipment today has proven incapable of preventing the constant jarring that causes long term brain injuries.

It is well past time to think of safer football alternatives, at least for the youth players. Flag football perhaps? How about the 7 on 7 summer passing leagues that seem to have caught fire at high schools across the country.

From a personal perspective I lament the state of what has become our national game. I played it, coached it at both the H.S. and college levels and still love to watch the weekly pageantry through the fall season each year. Would I play it and coach it today considering all that is known about jeopardy to our young people? In a word, "No".

JOE PATERNO

Much has been said in recent weeks about the life and contribution of the man known by many as Joe Pa. I was privileged to have known him personally over the years.

I met Joe Paterno in the winter of 1967 at the National Football Coaches Association meeting in New York City. In the fall of 1966 Joe and I were both new college head football coaches, he at Penn State and I at a small college in Iowa. That quirk of fate brought us together at a luncheon for new coaches on the second day of the convention. Joe was quiet at the luncheon table. I commented on his quietness and he put on that rye smile he often displayed and said, "We were just 5 and 5 this year so no one wants to hear what I have to say."

"The Joe Paterno I knew always seemed to come down on the side of the Angels."

A year later Penn State started a string of 22 straight victories and everyone wanted to hear from Joe Paterno. The next time we were together was back stage at the National Football Coaches Convention in Los Angeles a couple of years later when I had just finished a presentation. Joe was next up before the coaches but stopped to talk a minute before he went to the stage. He always treated me well when we were together. He said he had followed us through the year and noted that my team had led the nation in scoring. He said he wanted to talk to me later about what we were doing. That conversation never took place. Believe me, he didn't need help from anyone at that stage of his career.

Joe and I spoke several times until I left coaching in 1971. He was always a gentleman, soft spoken, and respectful. Unlike many, he returned his phone calls. Other coaches described him as quiet until the major issues were on the floor and then he would speak his mind. When he did, the issues were often resolved. Joe Paterno was always a voice for the better outcomes of collegiate athletics. He believed in the important values and always seemed to come down on the side of the Angels in any controversy.

The last time Joe and I were face to face was at the U.S. Olympic Delegate Assembly in Portland, OR when we both served as representatives. He grabbed my hand like a long lost brother and the conversation was as if we had never been apart. That was the kind of person he was, one who never lost a friend, one who treated everyone with warmth and respect.

Many believe that Joe Paterno should have done more regarding the controversy that cost him his job. In this situation I readily admit to being a Joe Pa defender. Here are a series of questions for those who believe that he was complicit in the Sandusky scandal. Had he gone to the police with the information told to him by a graduate assistant wouldn't that have been second hand, hearsay, gossip? Wouldn't Joe Paterno and the University have been liable for slander charges if his word couldn't be substantiated? Wasn't the proper thing to do to share the information with his Athletic Director and to urge the eyewitness to report it to the university authorities? Then, the university's investigative mechanism could work through the situation to find the truth. Didn't Joe Paterno, in fact, follow university procedure in reporting the incident to the administrative chain, in this case the Athletic Director.

In short, Joe Paterno made sure the next level of university administration had the potentially incriminating information. He did what he thought was right considering that he did not have first-hand knowledge. Unfortunately, the Athletic Director and Vice President dropped the ball and left Penn State University with a scandal of gigantic proportions, one that caught Joe Paterno in its aftermath and one that is not yet over.

By almost any standard Joe Paterno was an outstanding football coach, an outstanding representative for college athletics, and a fine man. To have his many achievements tainted by events that he did not initiate, was not complicit in, and was not guilty of in any way is, indeed, tragic. Joe Pa deserved better.

THE MOST WONDERFUL TIME OF THE YEAR ... FOR SPORTS FANS

Newspaper writers usually reserve that "most wonderful time of the year" title for the Christmas season. However, for sports fans the best time every year is the month that begins the middle of March and ends in mid-April. During that stretch of time we have March Madness featuring both the men's and women's basketball teams fighting it out for national supremacy. Major League baseball begins its new season the first couple of days in April, and the Master's Golf Tournament in Augusta is just around the corner. If you are a die-hard football fan, spring football is usually going on at your favorite school.

Football always occupies us from the fall into mid-winter. From then on, it is a buffet of different sports events.

Here in early April, March Madness is behind us with North Carolina taking home the men's trophy and South Carolina the women's. We are just at the beginning of baseball so no one's favorite team is more than a game or two below .500. Hope does spring eternal. By the time you read this the Master's Golf Tournament will be history and we will find out who stepped up for the win in the absence of Dustin Johnson, the favorite who had to cancel because of a back injury.

There is a first in NCAA championships that a citizen of South Carolina should point out. In the spring of 2016 Coastal Carolina University of South Carolina won the Collegiate Baseball World Series in Omaha. In the fall football season that culminated in the national championship game between defending champion Alabama and challenger Clemson University of South Carolina, it was the challenger who scored with six seconds on the clock to win the championship. Then, just a week ago the University of South Carolina Women's basketball team won a hard fought game with

Mississippi State to take home their first national championship.

The thought to contemplate is, "When have Universities from one state held national collegiate titles in the three major sports of football, basketball, and baseball at the same time?" The answer from the NCAA archives is........"Never."

"Wait till next year," is often the rallying cry when the home team does not do as well as the faithful wanted. So, what can we expect as we look ahead to the major sport seasons in the future?

First, Oregon is currently ranked number one in NCAA baseball rankings. However, the Atlantic Coast Conference has teams well placed with Louisville ranked number 2, Clemson 4, and North Carolina 5. We can expect that at least two of these will make it to Omaha to compete for major hardware in June.

Football season always occupies us from early fall into the winter schedule. Next year Alabama, always competitive, should be more so with stellar recruiting classes each year and a returning quarterback. Will Clemson be back to defend their 2016 championship? Stranger things have happened. An All-American quarterback has graduated but the overall talent is still on campus. Don't be surprised to see a third year rematch between these two college football powers.

Can North Carolina and South Carolina repeat as champions of men's and women's basketball? With major personnel loses to graduation and the professional ranks the odds are against it, but coaches Roy Williams for NC and Dawn Staley for SC are still in place and both are capable of producing yet another championship season.

Incidentally, would you call it "piling on," if I reported that Dustin Johnson, current top ranked golfer in the world, is from Columbia, South Carolina?

I confess to being a sports fan. Like most of my vintage, I played a bit of everything growing up. And, like most All-Backyard athletes I slipped easily into the spectator category as the years passed. Still, writing about it is a welcome relief from the national issues that are my usual focus.

12

JUST FOR FUN

If you just close your eyes for a moment and think "funny" you will come up with a dozen stories, pictures, or thoughts that made you laugh out loud in your not too distant past. We all have them. Too bad we can't conjure them up when we want to tell them to someone else. Too bad when we do, that the punch line always seems to be hiding somewhere in the deepest recesses of the mind.

Some comedians, Bob Hope as an example, made people laugh by his one line comments, one after another. Others, Jack Benny, for example, could make you laugh just by putting his hand up to his face and saying, "Well." Jerry Lewis regaled us with what came to be called, slap-stick comedy, using pratfalls and strange facial expressions. No one could match Red Skelton for catching you off-guard. One of his favorites was his depiction of the three stages of life. He said there was "youth," "middle age," annnnnnnnd "looking good."

Perhaps my favorite joke of all time is the one where the man parks his car in the church parking lot and walks by the marquis on the front of the church. It says, "If you are through with sin, come on in." Down in the corner, written in red lipstick it said, "If you aren't, dial 224-6542."

O.K., now think of your favorite. Is it a joke or a story that makes you smile? And, when is the last time you had a really deep "belly laugh?'

Read on, we guarantee a smile or two, and we just may make your day.

CELEBRATING BIRTHDAYS
WELL INTO YOUR EIGHTH DECADE

My wife does birthdays very well. She always has something special for every member of the family, and once a year whether I like it or not it's my turn.

When I was born my grandfather was 60 years old. I began to really get to know him when I was about 8. One thing I knew about him for sure was that he was really, really, really old, maybe one of the oldest people in the world. He was 68 that year. Today, I am that plus another half dozen. Now, there is sober realization.

My grandchildren are going to sing "Happy Birthday" to someone they think is really, really old. Hmmmmmmmm.

Still, if you've lived that long you must have learned some things that would be of value to the younger generation if you could only get them to listen. Let me share a few of my life's lessons. Maybe some young person will read this.

Everyone has TALENTS, special abilities that are uniquely yours. You have them, I have them, all of God's children have them. Some of the best advice I ever received was to "Find out what you are good at and see if you can get someone to pay you for doing it." One key to being happy in life is finding out which talents and special abilities you have and developing them.

DETERMINATION and its twin SELF DISCIPLINE are key factors in your ability to succeed in life. When you know what your talents are you need to apply a goodly amount of determination and self-discipline to pursue them. Professional athletes are found of saying, "Success is 10% inspiration and 90% perspiration". Writers are known to disappear for months at a time while they work at their craft. There is an illusion that you either have "it" or you don't. In truth, even people with lots of talent must work for months and years to perfect their talents before they can succeed. Talent without the determination and self discipline to succeed is wasted talent.

Everyone needs a PASSION. In this case I'm not talking about choosing your life partner. I'm talking about something that stirs your emotions and draws your interest. Some of our friends tell us their blood runs the color of this or that football team on a fall Saturday afternoon. My son is an attorney who makes his living in the world of insurance, but his passion is ping-pong. Yes, I said ping-pong, table tennis, the table game with the net and the little round ball. He loves the game. In his youth there was an age group national championship and a summer training camp at the U.S. Olympic Training Center in Colorado Springs before college and law school re-channeled his energy. Today, he still plays each week and it provides his physical conditioning and many of his personal friends.

I'm not sure it is possible to have a good life without having a goodly amount of FAITH. I could talk about faith in God and faith in things greater than we are as providing comfort and security for us. However, in this case I am talking about developing a strong and abiding faith in yourself. Someone smarter than me once said, "If you think you can or if you think you can't, either way you are probably right."

I'm not "big" on the concept of retirement. A few years back The Reader's Digest magazine ran a list of ten things to do or not do in order to have the best chance of reaching age 100. Number one on the list was "Don't Retire." One doesn't have to have a paying job but one does need a pursuit that fires the imagination and keeps the blood pumping.

Ahhh, birthdays. In a few weeks I'm going to hear my six grandchildren sing "Happy Birthday" to someone I'm sure they think is really, really, really old. And, I may be but I don't intend to act like it. Someday they will know the truth.

COMPUTERS ARE JUST TOO COMPLICATED

Most of my working life has been spent on a college campus. I have worked at colleges in five states, including Missouri, Iowa, Illinois, South Carolina and California. Like most of my vintage I prepared for my career before computers were invented. Even after computers became "necessary" on college campuses in the 1980s I had young people around me to make those mechanical marvels work their magic.

When I left the University to enter the world of international education it became obvious that I was going to have to master the computer so I could communicate with those on the other side of the globe. What followed was a trying time where my son, something of a computer guru, tried to teach me how to use a computer. I shall not soon forget the painful experiences that accompanied that learning process.

I am not sure people of my vintage are wired to master today's electronic equipment.

Whether it's a cell phone, VCR, or computer, I am not sure people of my vintage are wired to master today's electronic equipment. I know research has shown that the younger you are the easier it is to learn a second language. I think modern electronics has a language all its own and mastering it may take more "youth" than people in their 7th decade have to offer. I can remember my son standing at my shoulder saying, "Dad, do you want to learn this or do you just want to sit there and be mad?" In that process, no doubt, the son becomes the father and vice-versa.

My son lives in Rhode Island and one day I was on the phone with him trying to work through yet another computer problem. Twice we had been through his "simple" step by step directions. While I was struggling a young man who worked for us came in the side door. He stood just behind me as my son again tried to lead me through the process of solving the problem. As we failed the

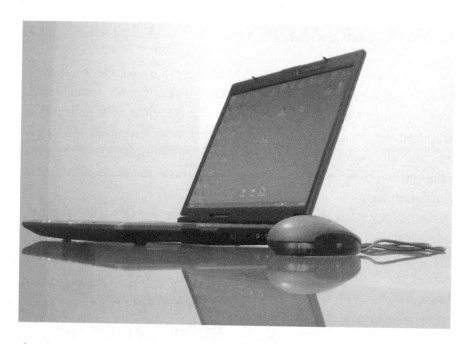

third time the young man spoke, "Dr. Hopkins". With just those two words my son, listening on the other end of the phone, said, "Who is that?" I told him. He said, "How old is he?" I told him he was fifteen. He said, "Put him on the phone." In about two minutes they had the problem solved. That young man was properly wired.

Nothing is hard to accomplish if you know how to do it. Unfortunately, there are areas of our modern world where experience may be our worst enemy. At the very least the electronic marvels of our time prompt us oldsters that our young people have something to contribute to us, no matter how painful the process might be.

MY BUCKET HAD SOME STARS IN IT

A while back I saw the movie, The Bucket List, with Jack Nicholson and Morgan Freeman. The story was about two men with terminal illnesses who had a list of things they wanted to do before they died -- before they "kicked the bucket," so to speak. I suspect that everyone has a "bucket list", either written or unwritten. This column is about one of mine.

Ruth and I spent a pleasant ten days recently visiting national parks in southern Utah. She reluctantly went along to help me check off four or five things on my bucket list. So it was Zion, Bryce, Canyonlands, Cedar Breaks, Dead Horse, and Arches National Parks on successive days. In truth, my real reason for going had to do with the National Parks designated dark areas in the country. Indulge me a few minutes for an old-timers story and you may understand better what was on my mind.

The memory of those summer nights has been in my mind for about 70 years now.

When I was growing up in southeast Missouri in the late 1940s, you could go out in your back yard, lie down in the grass and look up at the sky and see more stars than you could count. The Milky Way stretched from horizon to horizon and the Big Dipper was over there and Venus was the brightest star in the sky though it had hundreds of rivals. The memory of those summer night skies has been in my mind for about 70 years now.

Why only "in my mind?" Light pollution is such today that there are just a few spots in the country where you can see the Milky Way. All of those places are well west of the Mississippi. Bryce and Canyonlands National Parks are two of those places. I didn't really talk much about seeing the stars again as we prepared for the trip. Who could justify spending ten days and two thousand dollars to see some stars? Well, who indeed?

As luck would have it the day designated for Bryce Canyon

was overcast and spitting rain. The park gave up its sights but no night sky with the splendor of my memories. So, we headed across the state to the little town of Moab which sat between Canyonlands and Arches. After spending the day at Arches we had supper at a local restaurant where a young waitress suggested star gazing at a place called Ken's Lake south of town. We realized as we drove into the parking lot that we had entered what appeared to be the local lovers' lane. I wondered how the young lady knew that place so well.

We shut off the car engine, got out of the car and there it was. There was the memory. The Milky Way stretched from horizon to horizon with more stars than you could count. There was Venus, Polaris, and the Big Dipper so close you could almost touch them. Stars were everywhere by the millions. We counted a least four airplanes in the sky going somewhere, along with an occasional shooting star, probably falling space debris from all the junk we have shot up there over the past 60 years since the time of Sputnik in 1957. Amazing! Simply amazing!

The next evening we made our way to Dead Horse Point Visitor's Center at the edge of Canyonlands Park for a second night of watching God's celebration of the night sky. It was even better than the first night. As we drove out of the park we stopped for one more last look, probably the last time I will be able to renew that memory of summer nights 70 years ago.

There are many things still languishing on my bucket list but one by one I am checking them off. Seeing the night sky again in all of its magnificence was worth the trip and I would do it again in a minute.

SO, WHO IS GROWING OLDER?

Call me a wild and crazy guy (Yes I stole that line from Steve Martin.) but recently, on a whim, I decided to allow another birthday. I turned 78.

It's not so bad. Physically, the only serious problem I've noticed is that I can no longer read anything printed in letters smaller than SHAQUILLE O'NEAL. And, I can't hear anything that arrives at my ear lower than the sound from a near-by lightning strike.

The only serious thing I have noticed is that I can't read anything smaller than SHAQUILLE O'NEAL.

I suppose I should see an eye doctor and, yes, an ear doctor as well. However, I have become more than a bit leery of doctors since they always seem to want to insert a lengthy medical item into your body until the far end of it reaches a different area code.

Anyway, other than being functionally deaf and blind, I remain in superb physical condition for a man of my age who can no longer fit into any of his pants. That, despite a restrictive diet regimen of not eating any sweets before ten A.M. and exercising rigorously every Thursday between nine and nine thirty in the morning.

Because of my midriff situation I was very pleased to read recently about the new Miracle Breakthrough Weight Loss Plan ....for Mice. In case you missed it, what happened was, scientists extracted a certain chemical ingredient found in thin mice, then injected it into fat mice. The fat mice lost 10 per cent more weight than a control group of fat mice who were exposed only to watching Richard Simmons.

The good news is that this same ingredient could produce dramatic weight loss in humans. The bad news is that, before it becomes available, it must be approved by the Food and Drug Administration. Their motto is, "We haven't yet approved our motto." So, it's going to take a while.

But, getting back to the aging thing: Aside from the vision thing, the hearing thing, and the weight thing, and the need to take an afternoon nap almost immediately after I wake up from one, I am in pretty good shape. I have a steel trap for a mind. Of course, very few things in the world....and I include the Home Shopping Network in this statement....are as stupid as a steel trap.

What I'm saying is, though I am sure my mental capabilities are far superior to most, I have definitely detected a decline in some of my mental facilities. For example, I was attempting to fill out an IRS form the other day and I needed to divide 3 into $125.85, and I couldn't remember how to do long division. I knew I was supposed to put the 3 into the 12, then bring something down, but what? And, how far down? And, would I need the "cosine?' I was starting to panic when, all of a sudden, I knew exactly what to do. Ask Steve. Steve, is my son and he has a calculator.

I guess I need to get a calculator, and a magnifying glass, and a hearing aid, and some kind of device that remembers a) people's names, b) where I put the remote control, and c) what I had planned to do once I got into the kitchen during commercials.

So, my memory is going too. Well, I do remember this. When I was young there was no respect for youth. Now that I am old, there is no respect for age. It is sobering to realize that I missed it coming and going.

In truth, age is nothing more than experience, and some of us are more experienced than others. Yes, I am older this week than last but, I look better and feel better, and I'll tell you something else, I never lied better.

STILL LOOKING FOR MY SUPER POWERS

The local headline said, "Fans turn out for ComiCon." And so they did. They held a convention for comic book devotees where the participants turned up in costume. Just walking through the lobby one could see The Incredible Hulk, Wonder Woman, Super Man and a host of other comic book characters. There were lots of children but many adults too. Have you wondered why such fantasies attract full grown adults? I think I have an answer.

I was visiting at a neighbor's home the other day and his eight year old son come running through the room with a cape on, flying from room to room as you would expect from someone who has super powers. It didn't hit me until I was on the way home, I used to have super powers too.

> **Have you wondered why such fantasies attract full grown adults?**

All boys pass through a stage where they believe they have super powers. It usually hits between the ages of 6 and 10. Women believe these fantasies eventually fade and their men become real people. What women don't understand is that these aren't fantasies, what goes on in the mind of the male of the species is very real. How else could I account for the broken arm I received from flying off the roof of the garage? Men are born thinking they can leap tall buildings with a single bound or, if given the chance, could be the hero who saved the world. Ladies, your men have duel personalities too. How else could he be the hero your youngsters need to look up to and, at the same time, be unable to put a washer in a dripping faucet?

A friend of mine was reluctant to tell how he broke his ankle but finally confessed that he was showing his son how he used to dunk a basketball. In the process he hit his foot on the pole that holds up the goal. Zonk! Off to the emergency room. I sympathized with him but smiled inwardly as I remembered showing my daughter how to ride a skateboard. Zonk! Off to the emergency room.

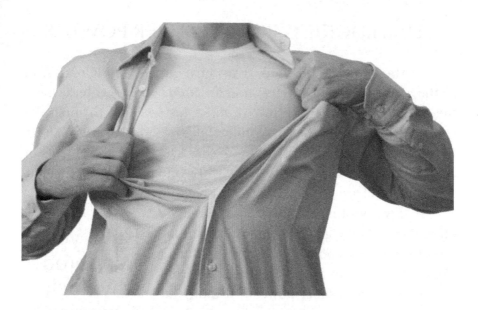

Still, who is going to show those things to our younger generation if not those of us who can call on our super powers from time to time?

So, considering that such powers do exist in the male of the species what happens to them over the years? There is a simple explanation. Our powers have been zapped by Kryptonite. Where is this Kryptonite? It is in the walls of the offices we work in and in the tools we have stored in the garage for whenever we need to save the day. It creeps in with sore shoulder and back pain, my wife's eyes that roll with disbelief, or my son simply stating with that telling tone of voice, "You're getting old Pop." It doesn't seem to suffice to say, "Well, I useta could."

THINGS WERE DIFFERENT THEN

Consider this relief from the news coming from Washington DC and North Korea in recent days. I thought you might like to hear about a recent conversation I had with a granddaughter.

She asked me what my favorite fast food was when I was growing up. I told her we didn't have fast food when I was her age. All the food was slow.

"C'mon, seriously. Where did you eat?" she asked.

"Well, McDonalds hadn't been created yet in my day," I replied. "Mom cooked every meal and we sat down together at the kitchen table. If I didn't like what she put on my plate I was allowed to sit there until I did like it. During the school year we carried our lunches in paper sacks. Mostly, it was liverwurst on crackers and, if we were lucky, peanut butter and jelly on bread. Milk was carried in a glass jar and sat on the window ledge to keep cool."

> **Mom cooked every meal and we sat down at the kitchen table together.**

Later, I thought about other things I could have told her about my childhood though I am not sure if her system could handle it.

Some families never owned their own house, never wore Levis, never set foot on a golf course, and never traveled anywhere they had to say in a motel. Who could afford such extravagance?

My mother never took me to soccer practice. That was mostly because we had never heard of soccer. We did meet on a daily basis in the summer with the other kids of the neighborhood for a baseball game. When we didn't get enough for a game we played an off-shoot of baseball we called Indian baseball. You could play it with three on a side. (I'm not really sure Indians ever played baseball.)

We didn't have a television or a car or a telephone while I was growing up. My grandmother had a television. It was black and white, and the station went off the air at midnight, after playing the National Anthem and a poem about God.

I was in college before I tasted my first pizza. When I bit into it, I burned the roof of my mouth and the cheese slid off, swung down, plastered itself against my chin and burned that, too. It is still the best pizza I ever had.

Pizzas were not delivered to our home, but milk was. All newspapers were delivered by boys. My older brother and I shared a paper route. We delivered newspapers six days a week. It cost 7 cents a paper of which we got to keep 2 cents. Mercifully, it was an afternoon route so we didn't have to get up at 6:00 a.m. every morning. On Saturday my brother had to collect 42 cents from the customers. His favorite customers were the ones who gave him 50 cents and told him to keep the change. His least favorite customers were the ones who never seemed to be home on Saturdays which meant he had to go back again and again until he could catch them at home.

Movies were the big attraction in our town. The local theatre changed class "B" movies on Friday, Sunday, and Wednesday. It cost 10 cents to get in and popcorn was 5 cents. They ran a serial with the movie to keep you coming back. Every one ended with a "cliff-hanger." There were no movie ratings because all movies were produced without profanity or violence or most anything offensive. When Clark Gable came out with that line, "Frankly, my dear, I don't give a damn," in "Gone with the Wind." it horrified the more gentile public. Preachers preached against the….."What is this world coming to?"…society, and some swore off of movies altogether. (Well, no one really swore in my day.)

Well, I knew before I started talking to her, she wouldn't believe it.

13

OTHER

One can create all the categories you can think of but there will still be Items that will defy categorization. Where would you put something about "Living Longer," or "Warning Signs?" So, every Table of Contents needs an "other" category to pick up the stragglers.

I suspect that is true of virtually everything we can think of. They say no two snowflakes are alike. For sure, no two people are alike. We have all known brothers or sisters, even twins, where one is several inches taller than the other. Some people can sing. Some can't. Those that can may be sopranos, or they may be tenors. Hair color? It comes with the genes. That is, unless it comes out of a bottle. My wife let her hair go gray. I would love to let mine go gray, but it disappeared a long time ago.

The point is that we are as individual as God could make us. We don't live the same way as others and, for sure, we don't age the same way. I have a friend who died twenty years ago. Actually, he is still up and walking around, but for all practical purposes he died in his sixties. Mentally, he was old before his time. I have another friend who is well into his 90s. He is still writing poetry and contemplating starting a writer's guild. My mother was that way. She died at 99, but she was still telling me what to do right up until she couldn't remember my name.

I love the attitude of the lady who said, "I don't ever want anyone to refer to me as a sweet, little old lady. Instead, I want them to always wonder what the old lady is going to get into next."

"Other" is a very good word. It means different or distinct, intrinsically different from something else.

So read on if you want to learn about some very different things.

ABOUT LIVING LONGER

This is a column about how to live to a ripe old age, to avoid Alzheimer's and a number of other ailments that afflict senior citizens. We are inundated with information about living a healthy life. Who doesn't know about keeping cholesterol and blood pressure in check, about avoiding fatty foods and keeping our weight down? Here is one I'll bet you haven't heard that showed up in a research study of more than 3600 men and women over the age of 50. The research came from the Yale School of Public Health and the University of Michigan's Health and Retirement Study.

Simply put, "Word power increased brain power."

First, do you read? The research study revealed that people who read books for as little as 30 minutes a day lived an average of two years longer than people who don't. Odder still, book readers who reported that they read more than three hours a week were 23 percent less likely to die in a given year than their peers who read only newspapers and magazines.

Recent studies on adult reading tell us that reading over a lifetime can support healthy brain function. Simply put, "Word power increases brain power."

So, what is it that makes reading books so developmental for our brains? Researchers believe that reading books, what they call "deep reading," forces the brain to think critically and to make connections from one chapter to another. When we make connections, chapter to chapter and character to character, the brain forces new pathways between regions throughout the brain. Over time this promotes quicker thinking and fights the effects of brain decline that comes naturally with age.

What else other than reading books helps us to live longer? Learning a second language is a major plus. Those who are proficient at a second language are stronger at multitasking, superior at memorizing, and better at focusing on important information that those who are stuck in one language. The younger a person can began to study a foreign language the more likely they are to master it. In learning languages beginning early is a great help. In my years of working with college personnel I have had many who could speak two or more languages. One lady could speak five Southeast Asian languages. I'm sure I didn't appreciate her nearly enough.

I think learning to use a computer is similar to learning a foreign language. Again, starting early is beneficial. The benefits, however, are the same whether you are younger or older.

Other major positives include learning to play a musical instrument and creating works of art. Being able to translate the music on the page into one's brain and hands is like learning a foreign language. The same is true with taking a clean canvas and filling it with artistic designs. In younger years I played the trumpet. I also tried piano, French horn, and the guitar. None of those took with me like the trumpet. I played taps at funerals, in H.S. and college bands, and for a while in a jazz ensemble. My wife, Ruth, is still known locally for her paintings.

It is true that I have a vested interest in urging people to read. I write a weekly column. I also have written seven books with an eighth almost finished. Still, the research is pretty convincing. If you read something and do it often it is good for the development of your brain. If you read books and do it for three to four hours each week that is even better.

We have multiple studies that tell us to keep our bodies fit. They promote walking, lifting weights, and exercising in a number of ways. All are important. However, no muscle in the body is as important as the brain that controls them all. A favorite teacher used to say, "A word to the wise should be sufficient."

IN PRAISE OF HARD WORK

Many in the older generations can tell stories of how hard it was growing up, working, and getting an education. That was back, "in the day." In the 1930s, 40s, and 50s it was usual for a young person to have at least a part time job. They worked on farms, in stores, mowing lawns, and so on. It was a time when every person had to accept some responsibility for the wellbeing of the family and needed to contribute something to the family income.

Today, our young people have heard stories of an aging grandparent who had to walk five miles to school every day in the snow, uphill both ways. They have heard hardship so often their eyes begin to glass over. Still, because they find our stories difficult to believe, that is no reason we shouldn't tell them. Hard work is a learning experience and is its own reward. It is a lesson young people must learn in order to be successful in life.

Do you know of anything of note ever accomplished without the overriding effort of hard work?

What are the themes of the "old timers" stories? Television? We didn't have one. A car? No. School? Yes, but "taught to the tune of a hickory stick." Believe it, it was really true.

The Bible says, "Deny yourself and take up your cross". When we put that into everyday words it has to do with self discipline and hard work. It speaks of unselfishness and commitment to something greater than ourselves.

The Bible doesn't have an "exclusive" on those words. We can find almost the same thing written in the teachings of Buddha, in the Koran written by Mohammad, and in the Little Red Book with the sayings of Chairman Mao Zedong of the Republic of China. All four sources tell us to think beyond ourselves, focus on commitment to others, and work hard. Do you know of anything of note ever accomplished without the overriding effort of hard work?

Ignacy Jan Paderewski, one of the greatest pianists the world has ever known, said that he never missed a day of practice and his sessions often ran on for hours. Michael Phelps talks about rolling out of bed every morning at half past five to swim laps for two hours before school. His sacrifice resulted in a shelf full of Gold Medals and a place in Olympic history. Computer genius Bill Gates dropped out of Harvard University and started his computer software company in a garage. He made his first computer out of spare parts from old radios and X-ray machines. His genius is legendary and his commitment and dedication has revolutionized the world's communications and information sharing. He still hasn't graduated from Harvard.

Mothers of recognized geniuses have often testified that another child in the family had the greater talent, yet the one who had the greatest determination and worked the hardest was the one who succeeded at the highest levels.

America has long been called the land of opportunity. That phrase, "land of opportunity" tells us that one has the opportunity to achieve much. It does not say that much will be given to us, or that if we live here we will be rich. It says, instead, that we have an opportunity. Those who become successful put forth the effort and the hours of labor. They deny themselves today's rewards and focus on goals that may be years away from fulfillment. They PLAN, they COMMIT, and they WORK.

When Pablo Casals, one of the world's greatest musicians, died at the age of 99, he was in his music room practicing. Almost 100 years old and still practicing. We have all heard it said "Ohhhh, if I had his talent, I would do wonders. No! The real answer to the old joke about a visitor to New York City asking, "How do I get to Madison Square Garden?" is, in fact, PRACTICE, PRACTICE, PRACTICE.

NEW RESPECT FOR NEWSPAPERS

Last week I attended the annual conference of the National Society of Newspaper Columnists. Each year according to their publication, 300 of the best columnist from across the country come together to talk about the science and art of sharing news and information. Before you get the impression that I am including myself among the 300 best in the country I want you to know that anyone with $250 could attend.

I had the privilege of meeting some celebrated writers from around the country including Pulitzer Prize winner Maureen Dowd, Brian McGrory, Editor-in-Chief of the Boston Globe, Jill Lawrence, Editorial Page Editor of USA Today, and Scott Spradling, Emmy Award-winning reporter, anchor, and political commentator often seen on CNN with Wolf Blitzer and Ted Kppel. The winner of this year's coveted Will Rogers Humanitarian Award was Suzzette Standling, a syndicated columnist from Milton, Massachusetts. My assessment of the members of the NSNC is that they are a down-to- earth group of highly skilled professionals.

The local newspaper is still the primary source of news all across the country.

It wasn't a surprise that the general consensus of the group is that the Internet has caused a major earthquake in the newspaper business. Today, many opt to read their news online and that cuts into the financial bottom line of the newspaper business. On-line readers lose the "flop-over" opportunities provided by actually holding your newspaper in your hand and letting your eyes "flop-over" to an article you never would have anticipated had you been searching online for what you want to read. A significant value of the newspaper is that it provides information to which we would not, otherwise, be exposed.

All across the country newspapers have attempted to deal with the financial short-fall by changing the format of the newspapers to save space or by consolidating with other newspapers and creating a "central" printing source. Consolidations create another concern of which most would not be aware. As more and more smaller newspapers face a declining bottom line financially, those newspapers are being bought up by larger and stronger organizations. That means that, potentially, the editorial policies of local newspapers are in the hands of a smaller and smaller group of people. One of the strengths of the newspaper in previous years has been its independence and ability to view local and national issues from a variety of different viewpoints. More consolidations mean, potentially, fewer independent viewpoints. That can't be good.

One of the major problems of small city newspapers is how to balance local and national news coverage. That is especially true in those areas away from the big cities. With a mobile population some newspaper readers have moved to their present locations from far-away places and enjoy reading about national happenings. Others look for local news and turn first to the homeowner section.

If I brought nothing else home from my sojourn to the National Society of Newspaper Column Writer's Conference I can tell you that change in the Newspaper business is on-going. We have seen much change in recent years and it continues to accelerate.

If you get the bulk of your news from TV, you have the headlines but little else. If you drive with the radio on, you generally get lots of commentary but little content. The local newspaper continues to be the primary source of news and information all across the country. It is the tie that binds, the catalyst, and often the motivator to get people involved in important things that effect everyday life in these United States.

Thomas Jefferson said, "Were it left to me to decide whether we should have a government without newspapers or newspapers without a government, I would not hesitate for a moment to prefer the latter."

Three days at the national conference gave me a new appreciation for our local newspapers and for those charged with the overwhelming responsibility to bring it to us 365 days each year. Folks, we are both privileged and spoiled.

PAY ATTENTION TO THE WARNING SIGNS

At the close of a November meeting several years ago a lady asked for permission to address the group. Her message was direct and pointed. She said, "I have no desire to attend any funerals over the next several months. I want you all to swear off of shoveling snow, pushing cars that have slipped off of the road, jogging in below freezing weather, and other activities that put your heart in stress. Last winter I attended three funerals of long-time friends, all of whom died shoveling, pushing, jogging and doing things they should have known better than to attempt. None of you are in the peak of condition so think before you do something dumb."

Winter is the time when the number of hearts attacks accelerate.

Her comments left us all speechless. She was right. We were all older and more sedentary than in earlier years. Winter is the time when the number of heart attacks accelerate. So, to everyone reading this column please do as the lady advised. "Please think before you do something dumb."

Heart attacks and strokes are the twin maladies of our society. They are the numbers one and two killers in the United States. Each year 715,000 people have heart attacks and 795,000 suffer strokes. Heart attacks kill more than 100,000 each year and strokes kill 140,000. Someone dies from a heart attack or stroke every 30 seconds. More deaths are attributed to heart attacks and strokes than all types of cancer combined. In addition, strokes are the leading cause of long term disability in the U.S.

Women used to think of themselves as exempt from such problems but not anymore. The latest statistics tell us that one in seven female deaths will occur as a result of a heart attack or stroke.

So, what are the symptoms we should be looking for? The list includes being overweight, not sleeping at night, bouts of fatigue, legs that swell from water retention, and being short of breath walking from the parking lot into the store.

Several years ago I was playing tennis with my regular Monday night group. In the midst of the first set I was not feeling right. I asked for some rest time between sets. About half way through the second set, I did something I had never done before. I left my three friends on the tennis court and went home. I took a couple of aspirin and sat down in my easy chair. The next morning I called the doctor's office and, mercifully, he had a vacancy. I thought he would give me a stress test. He said, "No, you already had your stress test on the tennis court." Instead, he sent me to a cardiac specialist who sent me directly to the local hospital for a catheterization. So, an hour later, I found myself lying on a gurney with a doctor looking across at me saying, "We have a problem."

At the end of her diagnosis she said, "So, do you want to go to Emory in Atlanta or Greenville for your open-heart surgery?" I chose Greenville and asked, "Should I go home and pack a bag?" She said, "Your wife can pack a bag and meet you at the hospital. I have already called the ambulance for you."

That was 17 years ago. It was an experience I will never forget and not one I would recommend. But, on the bright side, I have watched my grandchildren grow up, seen several graduations, and experienced a lot of life that might have disappeared had I not been so fortunate. Well, more than fortunate.....blessed.

So, it is the time of year for heart attacks and no one in your family wants to go to a funeral. A treasured teacher of mine used to say, "A word to the wise should be sufficient."

A ZOMBIE APOCALYPSE?

The commercial on TV showed a man checking his home owner's insurance coverage. He asked if it covered his air conditioner. The lady said "No, air conditioners are not covered." He asked, "What is covered?" She responded, "Floods, earthquakes, and a Zombie Apocalypse." What, you may ask, is a Zombie Apocalypse? To get an answer to that logical question it might be well to watch a TV show called, "The Walking Dead."

My concern is not a fictional TV show. It is, instead, the fact that we have a senior citizen population that is growing at a rate of thousands each day with no end in sight. I am concerned with an aging population that still has abilities that are not being fully utilized. We lament our younger generation not taking advantage of their educational opportunities. How about a healthy, well-educated citizenry with capabilities to spare just sitting and watching the world go by? Where did we get the idea that we should quit work and live off of the dole for the rest of our lives? I can guarantee you it isn't in the Bible.

We should strive to make what some nin-com-poop called, "the golden years," as productive as possible.

Dr. Ezekiel Emanuel published an article in the Atlantic Monthly entitled, "Why I hope to die at 75." His thesis was that those over 75 contribute little to society but take up an inordinate amount of the nation's health resources. He said, "The nation would be better off if they were dead." I have to admit, considering that I am well into my 8th decade, that I don't care much for Dr. Emanuel's thesis.

Dr. Emanuel may have forgotten that Winston Churchill was still Prime Minister of England at the age of 81, that Ronald Reagan was still president of the United States at 78, and Grandma Moses did her best painting in her 80's. Henry Kissinger just authored another book on politics and international relations, his twelfth. That Nobel

Peace Prize winner is now 94. Still, Dr. Emanuel does have a message for us that is worth considering, that of making our senior years as productive as possible.

A Zombie Apocalypse? Not a chance. However, senior citizens do have a responsibility to the world we live in. We can't let ourselves become Zombies living from day to day with no goals or ambitions that benefit those around us. All of us have time, energy, and abilities that can be utilized for the public good. The secret is to push out from our artificial boundaries and look for a place to serve.

Those of us who have reached what some nin-com-poop called the "golden years" should strive to make those years as productive as possible. There are numerous community organizations such as Meals-on-Wheels, Red Cross, and United Way that need volunteers to provide services to those less fortunate. Churches have become the backbone of what former President George H.W. Bush called "points of light" in our communities. They have a never ending list of opportunities for us to be of service to others. We just need to open our eyes to the possibilities. And, it goes without saying that the younger generation needs our wisdom and, even more, our example.

One compatriot from Keokuk, Iowa wrote me a few weeks back telling me about volunteering with first and second graders to improve reading skills and working with kids at The Son Valley Youth Ranch (Canton, MO). The opportunities are legion.

So, here is a challenge for you. Most of us are motivated by example and opportunity. If you are a senior still volunteering and doing good things for others, take a minute and write me a note. Let me know what you are doing. My E-mail is presnet@presnet.net. I will find a way to get many such E-mails into a future column. Share your example. We may stimulate some other seniors to look for new opportunities. The benefits may multiply.

SENIORS DOING FOR OTHERS

A few weeks back I wrote a column entitled, "Zombie Apocalypse." It related to my concern with the fact that at this time in history our population is aging significantly and every single day another 10,000 seniors slip past the coveted age 65 mark.

Dr. Ezekiel Emanuel published an article in the Atlantic Monthly entitled, "Why I hope to die at 75." His thesis was that those over 75 contribute little to society but take up and inordinate amount of the nation's health resources. He said, "The nation would be better off if they were dead." My "Zombie Apocalypse" column raised the question with seniors across the country regarding productivity of seniors in doing for others. The following is a sampling of their replies.

- In Adrian, Michigan a lady (77) tells me she continues to work for the Department on Aging.
- In Anderson, SC a senior involved in the AARP tax-aid program worked on more than 500 tax returns last year.
- Another South Carolina senior cites work with the League of Women Voters and services offered and forums held here and there in the region.
- A Hillsdale, Michigan lady, (83) still gives private piano lessons in her home.
- A man (97) drives for Meals on Wheels and tells me that his activity is usual among his friends in Bartlesville, OK.
- A lady from Northwest Florida serves on boards and advisory councils and still has time to write books on genes and genealogy.
- A senior couple from Florida cites Baptist Disaster Relief and help with "Mended hearts, Inc." a support group for those who have had open heart surgery.
- A lady from Imperial Valley, Calif., tells me she is a volunteer with the adult literacy program at their local library.
- An Air Force Veteran (84) volunteers at the USO and for the Caring Connections and Children in Crisis Ministries at her church.

- A lady from Crestview, Florida tells of a 92 year old friend who serves as a Master Gardener consultant.
- A lady in Ft. Walton Beach operates cold night shelters and food distribution for the homeless. Several of her friends provide services for the homeless.
- Another Florida lady tells me of her mother who serves as a member of the retired military officers Association and the Republican women's club.
- A Michigan lady, (84) talks of being a "field interviewer," for the U.S. Public Health Service. In other words, she knocks on doors and asks questions.
- A Michigan couple, ages 84 and 85, volunteer at their church and at the local hospital Emergency Room.
- One distant friend from Iowa volunteers at Son Valley Youth Ranch each month.

Phrases such as "wearing out is better than rusting out," and "use it or lose it," dotted the responses from seniors from all over the country.

I must admit I was not prepared for the volume of responses that came from the "Zombie Apocalypse," column. What I have shared in this column is just the tip of the iceberg. Not only are seniors all over the nation lending their expertise and services to a variety of community benevolences but they don't mind telling you about it and sharing stories of their many experiences.

I live in a community of 50,000 with a YMCA, public library, hospital, free clinic, meals on wheels, more than 40 churches, and 60+ United Way organizations that all need volunteer help. Many communities have performing groups who provide entertainment to seniors groups, nursing homes, and assisted living centers. The possibilities are endless.

If I was wondering what a senior will do in retirement I wonder no more. One just has to look over the possibilities and take that all important second step. Get out of the house and keep moving. Wasn't it Satchel Paige of the old St. Louis Browns baseball team who said, "Never look back, someone may be gaining on you"?

THE CONTRIBUTION OF GENIUS

I have always been fascinated with people who have worn the "tag" of genius. Most know about Physicist Albert Einstein and his Theory of Relativity and Medical Researcher Jonas Salk and his Polio vaccine. Inventors Thomas Edison, Alexander Graham Bell and the Wright Brothers revolutionized day to day living for all of us. Our business/industrial complex was shaped by Henry Ford, Andrew Carnegie, and John D. Rockefeller. In more modern times Bill Gates and Steve Jobs would certainly be included on the "genius" list for their work with computers which have ushered in amazing advancements in a variety of fields.

If you are not sure what I just said, don't feel bad, I'm not sure I understand it either.

Some had many inventions which we still use today, like Benjamin Franklin and Thomas Edison. Others focused on one field as Bill Gates did with computer software and James Harmon with electronic communications. What? You don't remember James Harmon? He revolutionized electronic communications by bouncing electronic waves off of the ionosphere. If you are not sure what I just said don't feel bad, I'm not sure I understand it either. But, we are all safer today because he figured out how our planes, tanks and ships could communicate over buildings, around mountains, and beyond the curvature of the earth. His patents include electronic marvels used in our international satellite systems. In short, because of his genius we can sit in our living rooms and watch the world go by and our military troops can keep in contact with their families from anywhere on the globe.

James Harmon grew up down the block from me in a rural Missouri town and went to college just up the road in a small state college. He got his start in his father's furniture store working on electrical appliances when he was a teenager in the 1950s. We had the same science teacher in H.S. and used to ride back and forth to college together. That is as close as I will ever get to genius.

Have you ever wondered what motivates and stimulates the minds of those who have created the world we live in today? Thomas Edison, who gave us the phonograph, the movie camera, and the electric light bulb among dozens of other inventions, worked in a think tank with several other inventors. By contrast, Mark Zuckerberg, created Facebook in a dormitory room motivated mostly by a girlfriend with whom he was angry. His first effort was a game he created that put two photographs side by side and asked others to identify them as "hot or not". One assumes that his former girlfriend didn't fare well in that comparison.

Over the past several years much of our national energy was focused on the problems caused by our recession. Would it surprise you to know that many of the major innovations that have improved our lives were created during times of recession?
Bill Gates dropped out of Harvard and began working on his Microsoft idea in 1976 at the age of 21. Three years later when he began to perfect his technology, we were in the depths of a recession that lasted well into the 80s. By the time that recession ended Gates was well on his way to revolutionizing the computer world. He created a new approach to international communications and provided the methodology that allowed us to evaluate research data at much more rapid speeds than had previously been possible. Steve Jobs honed his expertise during the same time period. The inventions and innovations of both Gates and Jobs have changed the world we live in forever.

It is said that "Necessity is the mother of invention". Assuming that is true, then "Recession" must certainly be its father. We have learned to expect some good to come out of any recession in the form of new inventions and innovations. Those effected most by a recession may follow the direction of John F. Kennedy and "dream of the impossible and say, Why not?" It is the genius dreamers who will contribute to the future for all of us.

WHEN THE CHIPS ARE DOWN YOU CAN COUNT ON AMERICANS

In Proverbs of the Old Testament it says "Pride goeth before destruction." Still, no matter where I go in the U.S. or anywhere else in the world I continue to carry a goodly amount of Pride in America. And, I don't feel any guilt about having that feeling.

The newspapers are full of the refugee crisis in Europe. More than three million people fleeing the war-torn cities of Syria are caught in a maze of confusion as they search for safety and security wherever they can find it. In the midst of this crisis who is helping? Who is on the scene with the necessities of life? Whether it is a refugee crisis in Europe, an earthquake in Haiti, or a volcano in Peru it is the people of the United States of America who arrive on site, "the firstest with the mostest," as my father used to say.

Whenever there is a crisis, there we go again, doing all we can against unbelievable odds.

In almost every crisis, four out of five aid workers, medical doctors, fire and rescue personnel on the ground working with the people are from the U.S.

We have our flaws as a country, for sure. Even now we have a homeless population of several million people and a full quarter of our children are not covered by health insurance. One would think that a country founded on the nobility of sacrifice and the blessings of the Almighty could do better. But, just when we begin to get frustrated with ourselves about our own shortcomings, here comes another international tragedy and there goes an invasion of Americans who suddenly appear with picks and shovels, white coats and stethoscopes, hot food and encouragement. This didn't start just last month, though we tend to forget each time until the next.

When a crisis hits our people begin to move toward the trouble. Doctors Without Borders, an American idea of the late 1960s, has been traveling the world for more than forty years taking care of the sick. In times of crisis our navy sends air craft carriers that carry on-board hospitals and food to desperate people wherever the need is greatest. The Carter Center in Atlanta, Georgia has been providing medical expertise in a number of third world countries since the early 1980s? Among their great successes is the near eradication of Guinea Worm Disease which formerly affected more than three million people a year and now is down to fewer than 200. Other major projects they are working on include the eradication of Mumps, Measles, and several other infectious diseases.

Let's review. Who created for the world the United Nations that still makes its home in New York City? Under its umbrella are The UNICEF and The World Bank who share benevolent services and money with countries around the globe? Who provided the money and the expertise to rebuild all of Europe and Asia following the great wars? Who leads the world in providing humanitarian aid after earthquakes and hurricanes? Who created benevolences like Hospice, Red Cross, United Way, and Community Crisis Centers all funded by local donations? Whose people give such great amounts in charitable donations to the worthwhile causes of the less fortunate? Who indeed? The people of the United States of America, that's who. The country built on the great ideal. The country that continues to fall short of its promise but is head and shoulders above every other country that ever existed in taking care of the needs of hurting people around the globe. When the chips are down, you can count on Americans.

Watch the news reports. Wherever there is a crisis, there we go again, doing all we can to help against unbelievable odds. Sense the desire to help and the frustration of the failures, but feel the pride in country and a people who, once again, reach into their pockets and into their hearts to help those in greatest need. Can you feel it?